JB JOSSEY-BASS™
A Wiley Brand

63 Winning Fundraising Strategies

Terrific Ideas for Meeting Your Goal

Scott C. Stevenson, Editor

WILEY

978-1-118-69067-3   ISBN

978-1-118-70386-1   ISBN (online)

63 Winning Fundraising Strategies
Terrific Ideas for Meeting Your Goal

Published by

Stevenson, Inc.
P.O. Box 4528 • Sioux City, Iowa • 51104
Phone 712.239.3010 • Fax 712.239.2166
www.stevensoninc.com

TABLE OF CONTENTS

63 Winning Fundraising Strategies

Terrific Ideas for Meeting Your Goal

TABLE OF CONTENTS

63 Winning Fundraising Strategies: Terrific Ideas for Meeting Your Goal.
Edited by Scott C. Stevenson.
© 2011 Stevenson, Inc. Published 2011 by Stevenson, Inc.

63 Winning Fundraising Strategies

Terrific Ideas for Meeting Your Goal

1. Be Creative in Offering Donor Incentives

What incentives do you offer to motivate your donors? At Hampden-Sydney College (Hampden Sydney, VA), a prize drawing is grabbing the interest of current and potential donors.

"We recently started offering a drawing for a monthly prize to encourage our Society of Founders members to give early in the year," says Mandalyn Thompson, assistant director of annual giving. "Every June there is always a big rush of last-minute gifts right before our fiscal year deadline. We wanted to encourage our donors to give early, and we wanted to do that in a way that would add to their experience as members of the Society of Founders."

In the contest, when someone makes a gift at the founders' level ($1,500-plus for all but recent graduates), or starts monthly payments on that level, that person becomes eligible for the drawing from that month to the end of the fiscal year.

In determining prizes, Thompson says, she and her colleagues looked beyond the typical ball caps or T-shirts because they wanted the prize items to be of considerable worth to those eligible for the drawing. They have included things like school logo cuff links and dinner with the college's president as prizes.

The prize drawing has donors and potential donors talking.

"We have received many positive responses about the new program," Thompson says, "along with e-mails from people asking if they are eligible or what they can do to become eligible."

Source: Mandalyn Thompson, Assistant Director of Annual Giving, Hampden-Sydney College, Hampden-Sydney, VA. Phone (434) 223-6149. E-mail: mthompson@hsc.edu

2. Tribute Tree Program Roots College in Its Past

With environmentally conscious moves taking center stage, now is the perfect time to launch a tree-planting campaign to benefit your nonprofit.

Hastings College (Hastings, NE) has a long tradition of tree planting beginning with the first spring planting season in 1883, says Matt Fong, director of alumni development. Through a new Tribute Tree program, Fong says, friends of the college can help that tradition continue.

The program began when fundraising efforts were wrapping up for the college's new science building. Fong says, "We were looking for ways to build the greenscape and let people continue giving." Here's how the program works:

Donors make a $500 donation to the program. In return, the college plants a tree of the donor's choice, selected from a predetermined list, and orders a plaque for the tree, which includes the type of tree and the name of the person being

Content not available in this edition

honored or memorialized. The donor's name and a tribute quote can be included on the plaque. Donors are encouraged to attend the tree-planting ceremony and bring family members with them.

To ensure success in the planting and growing process, the college's physical plant department works with a dedicated Professor Emeritus and the state Arboretum to determine which trees will thrive in the Nebraska climate. In addition, all trees that are planted are somewhat more mature trees, ranging six to nine feet in height. If, even with all these safeguards, the tree fails to thrive, Fong says the college will replace it if necessary, "though we may make a different suggestion about the type of tree or the location if it doesn't work after a few attempts."

The majority of the funds raised go to the college's Arboretum account so the greenspace can be maintained.

While only 10 to 20 trees have been purchased so far, the program is generating much interest, Fong says, especially after the college's recent tree-planting re-enactment. Even without that, Fong says he expects the program to catch on. "Campuses are beautiful, natural settings. People are interested in things that beautify the campus and live for a long time."

Source: Matt Fong, Director of Alumni Development, Hastings College, Hastings, NE. Phone (402) 461-7786. E-mail: mfong@hastings.edu

3. Committee of 100 Generates $50,000

Want to generate more $500 gifts for your annual fund? Here's one idea:

1. Initiate an exclusive annual gift club for anyone willing to make an annual contribution of $500 and give it a name such as The Committee of 100.

2. Anyone who gives at that level gets the privilege of voting how they wish to have their donations used based on recommendations from staff. Committee members choose how they wish their donations to be spent.

3. To increase membership in your Committee of 100, send an appeal directed to a targeted group of would-be donors and/or coordinate a phonathon. In addition, host special receptions for key individuals in your community that includes a brief program outlining the committee's goals.

If successful, your Committee of 100 will result in $50,000 in gifts directed to a funding project (or projects) that the group has collectively chosen.

4. Award Dinner Raises Significant Funds, Celebrates Leaders

Major annual events can bring awareness and valuable publicity to your mission while connecting you to people capable of providing significant financial support.

The 47th Annual Leaders in Management Award Dinner hosted by Pace University (New York, NY) on April 29 at the New York City

The award dinner was featured in a nationally distributed press release, in online event calendars such as New York Social Diary, Charity Benefits and BizBash Masterplanner, and gossiped about by Rush & Molloy of the NY Daily News.

landmark, Cipriani Wall Street, raised $605,000. The money will support Pace's student scholarship program, president-selected projects and general purposes.

"The proceeds from the event will count toward Pace's seven-year, $100 million Centennial Campaign goal, which we realized two months ahead of schedule," says Christine Meola, Pace's vice president for philanthropy.

The event, an annual tradition since 1962, celebrates the personal and professional accomplishments of industry and community leaders as well as the university's continued advancement and promising future, Meola says. "It also reunites alums and showcases our talented musical theater students, who have performed for each of the past three years."

This year's dinner honored magazine publishing magnate and alumnus David J. Pecker and online advertising innovator Gurbaksh Chahal.

Presenting Pecker's award was long-time friend and business associate Donald Trump. Presenting Chahal's award was Bruce Bachenheimer, clinical professor of management, director of entrepreneurship and Wilson Center for Social Entrepreneurship Faculty Fellow, who first met Chahal when he asked him to speak at a university event.

The celebration drew 325 attendees, including Eric Hillman, CEO of Europa Sports Products and an American Media advertiser, whose table included several noteworthy television celebrities. CNBC Anchor Maria Bartiromo served as mistress of ceremonies.

Tickets for the black-tie event ranged from $250 for young alumni level to $750 for contributor, $1,250 for supporter and $2,500 for sponsor. Sponsor table packages ranged from $10,000 to $50,000. Registration included the option of making a contribution if the person was unable to attend.

The event began with regular and VIP receptions at 6 p.m. Dinner was at 7 p.m. "Each presenter introduced a video of the honoree's career," says Meola. "For Gurbaksh Chahal, an excerpt from his interview with Oprah was shown (http://video.yahoo.com/watch/3791663/10391122) including the part where Oprah refers to him as 'one of the youngest and also the wealthiest entrepreneurs on the planet Earth.'"

To promote the dinner, Pace officials nationally distributed a press release by BusinessWire, says Samuella R. Becker, assistant director of public information. The event, Becker says, "was also featured on online event calendars such as New York Social Diary, Charity Benefits and BizBash Masterplanner, and gossiped about by Rush & Molloy of the NY Daily News. The San Francisco Chronicle also profiled Mr. Chahal in a story that appeared on the front page of one of its sections, entitled 'Internet Star Chahal Getting Honorary Doctorate.' We received requests for after the event photos."

Sources: Samuella R. Becker, Assistant Director of Public Information; Christine M. Meola, Vice President for Philanthropy, Pace University, New York, NY.
Phone (212) 346-1095 (Becker) or (212) 346-1637 (Meola).
E-mail: Sbecker2@pace.edu or cmeola@pace.edu

5.

Look to Social Media to Expand Your Fundraising Reach

Social media is one of the trendiest ways nonprofits can raise funds. But with your budget and staff already stretched how can you implement social media into your efforts?

"It's very important for nonprofits to be involved in social media, particularly because it's the wave of the future."

Take a cue from Big Brothers Big Sisters of America (BBBS), a Philadelphia, PA-based nonprofit that uses many social media venues. Here, Cheyenne Palma, director of development, shares what works for the organization:

Twitter (www.twitter.com) is one of the largest online social networking sites, and it's easy to get lost in all the tweets. How do you use this site productively?

"We try to tweet once a day during the work week. We only follow legitimate people who follow us (trying to avoid the spammers), and we also follow up with a direct message to further engage new followers."

Facebook (www.facebook.com) is another site that is seeing exponential growth. How does your Facebook fan page work for you?

"We have 4,035 fans, an increase of more than 40 percent for the year and our Facebook Causes site (a part of Facebook that allows 501(c)(3) organizations to receive donations through Facebook) currently has 1,896 members who have donated $613. To keep the fan page current and reduce time spent on it, we simply integrated our RSS feed into the site. We've also learned much of our current donor base is active on Facebook and through research and data analysis, we have located nearly 20 percent of them on the site. We've recently formalized our efforts to invite them to connect with us on Facebook."

LinkedIn (www.linkedin.com) is known more for its corporate network and as a place for like-minded business people to connect. Do you feel nonprofit fundraising has a place on LinkedIn?

"We are still in the very early stages of determining how we will use LinkedIn. We've begun to identify board members and donors who are active on LinkedIn, but have yet to complete this analysis. We have discussed using the Events module and the Groups functionality to connect with specific donors and supporters on LinkedIn. We anticipate this will be a much more targeted effort and not as broad an approach as Facebook."

It seems that cell phones can do just about everything now, including depositing paychecks online. Will BBBS dip its toes in the mobile giving waters?

"We are now piloting the ability to donate funds via texting and we have 11 agencies testing text giving. Primarily, we are testing its usage at local events, such as radiothons and baseball games. It appears there is potential where we have a very large, captive audience. Our East Tennessee affiliate received 83 donations in response to a recent radiothon in their market.

"We also anticipate folding mobile giving into our social media fundraising efforts through fundraising widgets. By placing a text-giving widget on select sites, viewers won't even need to go to a separate donation page to contribute; they can simply send a text."

What do you think is important for nonprofits venturing into social media to remember? And if they're not already doing it, should they be?

"It's very important for nonprofits to be involved in social media, particularly because it's the wave of the future. If you look at future generations of donors, it's how they communicate.

"An exaggerated example of this was demonstrated in a news article I read online recently about two teenage girls in Australia trapped in a storm drain — they updated their Facebook status instead of dialing for help! This is the future donor base that fundraisers are looking at tapping into; they need to get on board now, even if it's just to get their name and their message out there.

"Even from a budgetary perspective it makes sense: a few personnel hours per week can lead to donations that you might not otherwise have received, and there's no outside overhead to set it up or maintain it if you do it all in-house."

Source: Cheyenne Palma, Director of Development, Big Brothers Big Sisters, Philadelphia, PA. Phone (215) 665-7765. E-mail: cheyenne.palma@bbbs.org

6. ## Secure 100 Percent Staff Involvement in Fundraising

Many potential donors look at staff giving as a sign of an organization's overall success. After all, a staff that is invested financially is also invested emotionally.

Fontbonne University (St. Louis, MO) has successfully secured 100 percent faculty and staff participation in annual institutional fundraising, according to Marilyn Sheperd, vice president of institutional advancement. Since July 2007, Sheperd reports, every one of the 200 faculty and staff has contributed to the current campaign, with gifts totaling $250,000 to date.

The campaign to involve staff began in tandem with a major $20 million campaign in 2006. Sheperd and her gift officers began barraging faculty and staff with solicitations for contributions, just as they would major donors. They sent e-mail blasts, included advertisements in campus mailings and made announcements at all-campus meetings.

The most effective technique when asking staff for gifts? The same as when asking major donors, Sheperd says: face to face.

"We visited the night staff with coffee and donuts," she says. "At the all-campus meetings, when new staff and faculty introduced themselves, I was there with my pledge cards. The development staff also tried to give their staff/faculty the same kind of meaningful gift opportunities they would give to any outside donor, including the chance to honor a student or a special program."

While some staff gifts are quite modest, Sheperd says that with everyone giving, the entire campus feels part of the campaign. To celebrate the 100 percent participation goal, Sheperd commissioned a photo that shows all staff and faculty standing behind a huge sign reading "We Did It! 100%!" The photo has been used to celebrate and share the accomplishment and included in a donation brochure aimed at alumni.

Source: Marilyn Sheperd, Vice President of Institutional Advancement, Fontbonne University, St. Louis, MO. Phone (314) 889-4701. E-mail: msheperd@fontbonne.edu

7. ## Increase Major Giving With a Targeted Subcommittee

Volunteer fundraiser Kristy Hall took it upon herself to issue a challenge to One Home Many Hopes (OHMH), Sharon, MA, a small, start-up charity where she volunteered. Her challenge? Raise $20,000 in 30 days.

The effort would jumpstart the nonprofit, which raises money for Mudzini Kewtu, a home for abandoned and orphaned girls in Mtwapa, Kenya. Founded in November 2007, One Home Many Hopes had raised $4,000 and built a donor database of 150 in its first year.

While Hall's challenge seemed like a stretch, she actually succeeded well beyond that goal, bringing together a group of fellow volunteer fundraisers to raise $50,000 and increased One Home Many Hopes' donor database to more than 1,000 names.

One of Hall's key tricks to success was to divide her pool of fundraising volunteers into two subcommittees: one to solicit donations in the very low, $10 range, and a second subcommittee that went after much larger, $1,000 donations.

Hall recognized methods to approach the two groups would differ greatly. A major donor would want more information about where the money is going — not just to what nonprofit, but to what specific operational aspect of the nonprofit. A major donor would also want to know his/her personal values were being reflected in the nonprofit's work.

While the two subcommittees operated in some ways that were different, Hall also employed organizational methods that worked well for both of them:

❑ Forming a PR unit with additional volunteers increased media coverage, a universal approach that led to additional donations both major and minor.

❑ Scheduling a series of regular conference calls which helped to keep everyone motivated and informed of where they stood in relation to their target goals.

❑ Crafting a personal and unique pitch to donors that made OHMH stand out in the crowd among potential donors big and small.

Says John Boit, a fundraising volunteer and member of OHMH's board of directors: "We did all this in the worst economy in 80 years, with an unknown organization, in an incredibly short time frame, and at a moment when we were competing with every other organization in the world looking for year-end donations. Oh, and we didn't have a single paid person on staff — all were volunteers, working during lunch breaks and after work."

Thanks to Hall's efforts, OHMH is now a fully registered 501(c)(3) and has moved on to its next fundraising strategy: mining its donor database to encourage people to give small amounts on a recurring basis, including asking persons in the $1,000 donor level to provide the group with more financial security with smaller amounts of philanthropy.

Source: John Boit, Member, Board of Directors, One Home Many Hopes, Sharon, MA. Phone (617) 230-2574. E-mail: jboit@melwoodglobal.com

8. Y'ALL Campaign Reaches Out to Young Alumni

Development staff at the University of South Carolina (Columbia, SC) created a young alumni program to instill the importance of philanthropy in recent graduates.

Steve Farwick, assistant director of annual giving, answers questions about the Face of Y'ALL (Young Alumni Leaving a Legacy) campaign:

Please describe the Face of Y'ALL program.

"We launched the Face of Y'ALL, a first-of-its-kind campaign targeted toward Columbia campus graduates of the last decade. Young alumni are the future of the university, after all, and Carolina wants graduates' voices to be heard, while also helping classes of the last 10 years leave a legacy at their alma mater.

"We've discovered many recent graduates don't fully understand that tuition and state assistance are not fully covering the cost of an education. We want them to be aware of the fact that a considerable number of alumni and friends were passionate about supporting their education.

"A 12 percent campaign response rate exceeded our expectations for the Face of Y'ALL.... Nearly 1,600 recent alumni submitted updated biographical information, 139 applied to be the Face of Y'ALL and almost 1,000 voted for their favorite once the pool was narrowed down to five by a university committee. Once all the votes were tallied we ended with two fantastic representatives for our young alumni base."

What role have these "faces" played? What activities have they been involved in?

"Our two winners, Joey and Emily, are invited to the president's pre-game parties, given special privileges at football games, enjoyed a shopping spree at the university bookstore and are VIP guests at receptions and other university events. Most importantly, Joey and Emily are assisting with the creation of a Young Alumni Advancement Council (that) will help graduates of the last decade become better educated about the importance of philanthropy, share the university's mission with peers, promote participation and select marketing materials for their constituency. Joey and Emily will co-chair the council."

From a development standpoint, why was the campaign started?

"To help create philanthropic awareness and encourage participation in giving among our most recent graduates. Too often, universities focus on alumni who meet certain gift levels or other qualifications. We saw a great opportunity, despite a lower short-term return on investment, with our newest alumni. Educating them now through the Web, e-mail, direct mail and call center is paying off in huge dividends. The Y'ALL campaign has allowed us to communicate with this age group as we wouldn't other alumni constituencies.

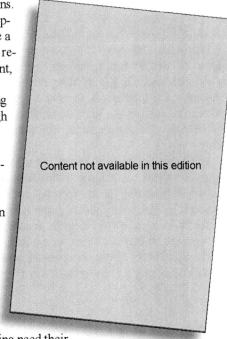

Content not available in this edition

Why does Carolina need their support? Is participation really more important than dollar amount given? Collectively, how can recent graduates make a difference? These are just some of the topics we address throughout the entire campaign. It's pivotal that these young alumni know they are the future of their alma mater in more ways than one."

What are the goals of the Y'ALL campaign?

"Engaging graduates of the last decade, educating them about the important role they play as alumni donors, having them serve on volunteer boards, carrying the university's momentum across the nation, serving their alma mater with pride and ensuring young alumni stay connected to Carolina. As we continue the program, we create even more awareness about philanthropy and the university as a whole. Since launching the campaign, the number of donors from the young alumni segment has increased by 16 percent. So far this fiscal year, the majority of online gifts are from this particular group as well."

Source: Steve Farwick, Assistant Director of Annual Giving Programs, University of South Carolina, Columbia, SC. Phone (803) 777-2592. E-mail: sfarwick@mailbox.sc.edu

9. ## Calendar Project Raises Eyebrows While Raising Funds

What do you call an auto dealer standing naked except for a strategically placed hubcap? Or a real estate agent enjoying a cigar and glass of wine with nothing more than a For Sale sign for cover?

The Greater Westerly-Pawcatuck Chamber of Commerce (Westerly, RI) calls it fundraising.

"They're all chamber members and basically naked except for a prop representing their business to cover their 'business,'" says Lisa Konicki, chamber executive director, of the chamber's popular Men of Westerly calendar fundraiser. "They get some great publicity, they help the chamber, and they raise money for some good causes, too."

The fundraiser, now in its second year, is planned and produced by the chamber, but proceeds are shared with several local charities, adding to its appeal and area impact. The 2010 calendar features 33 local businessmen of all shapes and sizes ranging in age from late 20s to early 70s.

"It's not about physical appearance," says Konicki, recalling the standing ovation received by the calendar's two over-70 models. "Featuring people with a solid reputation in the community, guys everybody knows and loves, is what really makes it work."

Because models are sworn to secrecy and photographed outside normal business hours, speculation fuels much of the buzz surrounding the event. A gala event — Men of Westerly Revealed — taps this curiosity with a grand reveal of the participating businessmen and an unveiling of the new calendar.

"Done right, it's something the community can really get behind," Konicki says, noting that 2009 calendar sales, combined with ticket sales, sponsorship and advertising, netted around $13,000. "It's fun, humorous and all about having a big heart."

Source: Lisa Konicki, Executive Director, The Greater Westerly-Pawcatuck Chamber of Commerce, Westerly, RI. Phone (800) 732-7636. E-mail: Lkonicki@westerlychamber.org. Website: www.westerlychamber.org

10. ## Holiday Fundraiser Raises Awareness for Organization

For the fourth year in a row, the hospice organization Gateway House of Peace (Greenfield Center, NY) presented its annual Light of Love Memorial Tree Lighting, which raises about $2,000 a year while generating awareness and friends for the organization.

The event is great for community outreach, says Joni Hanchett, president/founder. "It really motivates people to get involved with the organization."

The event takes place the first Saturday of December every year at The Barn at Mallery Street Marketplace, which helps sponsor the event by donating the laminated name tags and the tree. Four local businesses sell remembrance name tags for $2 each. Tags can also be purchased by mail. The day of the event, name tags are placed on the tree following Christmas carols by the local theater guild, an introduction of the organization and a prayer by a pastor from the community. Then, the tree is lit, followed by a reading of the names.

The biggest challenges of an event such as this, she says take place the first year of the event, when it is necessary to determine the size of event you want and how much to charge for the tags, among other things. "The first year is the most time consuming. Once you have your venue, flier, donation letter and event program in place, the next year is much easier."

Hanchett's best advice for those just starting out is to get

Luminary Sales Boost Proceeds

Selling luminary kits can be a cost-effective way to raise awareness and funds, says Joni Hanchett, president/founder, Gateway House of Peace (Greenfield Center, NY). The hospice organization hosts an annual Light of Love Memorial Tree Lighting.

"Luminary kits can be donated, costing the organization nothing," Hanchett says. "Restaurant distributors can donate white bags and your local town garage can contribute sand. After that, you will just need baggies and candles to complete the kits. In my research, I have found the going price to be about $10 for eight luminary kits. Local businesses can sell the luminaries for your organization, keeping it simple."

She adds that hospice officials plan to sell luminary kits during the annual Victorian Stroll in a neighboring town.

in on an existing event that already has a following and keep the name tags at a reasonable price, which encourages people to buy more than one tag.

Source: Joni Hanchett, President/Founder, Gateway House of Peace, Greenfield Center, NY. Phone (518) 893-6443. E-mail: jhanchett@gatewayhouseofpeace.org

11. Name-the-species Program Generates Funds, Awareness

What makes your organization unique? Incorporate those characteristics into your fundraising options and watch your support grow.

When Scripps Institution of Oceanography (La Jolla, CA) lost state funding for its Scripps Oceanographic Collections five years ago, staff and supporters tried raising money the traditional way, but found it challenging, says Lawrance Bailey, senior director of development.

"A collection of millions of biological and geological marine specimens is important, but not the sexiest or most exciting thing to donate to," says Bailey.

The idea for Scripps' Name-the-species Program came from Greg Rouse — a collections curator who serves on the Scripps Collections Task Force — and a group of volunteers and staff formed to raise funds for the collections. (Bailey notes that every year, Scripps' collections staff and researchers discover new species of marine creatures.)

"At first, we were thinking of (offering the naming rights) at an auction during an event, and were waiting for the right event," Bailey says. They had featured the name-the-species program in an internal newsletter, and while the article didn't generate much of a response, it triggered a follow-up story by a journalism student at Columbia University who posted her story on a website. In late March, a reporter from the San Diego Union-Tribune heard about the program and contacted Scripps, Bailey says. "She ran the story in early April, and our communications office did a press release immediately afterwards."

Bailey says they got the first inquiry call and the first donation shortly after that and have since received two other donations.

An Associated Press reporter picked up the story and did an article that ran in more than 200 locations a few weeks later, he says. Since that time, "we're continuing to get inquiries about the story, and are in discussions with a donor to name a deep sea fish, a species of Photonectes."

They have so far raised $45,000 toward building an endowment of $12 million.

Bailey says the primary benefit of the program has been its ability to raise awareness of the collection's existence and need for support: "We have this incredibly valuable collec-

tion that is an extraordinarily valuable resource for research and education," he says. "We want people to know that we are here, are valuable and need support."

The cost to name one of Scripps' newly discovered species ranges from $5,000 to $100,000 and depends on the variety of the species, its size, its appeal and the time it takes to identify it as a new species, says Bailey.

Donors who name a species receive a print of their named organism, as well as a copy of the scientific publication in which it is first described. The species naming process typically takes a year or longer to complete, he says, as the scientific process of careful research, paper submission and review for publication is very involved.

Source: Lawrance Bailey, Senior Director of Development, Scripps Institution of Oceanography, University of California, San Diego, La Jolla, CA. Phone (858) 534-7171. E-mail: lbailey@ucsd.edu

> "We want people to know that we are here, are valuable and need support."

Current Species Naming Options

Species currently available to be named at the Scripps Institution of Oceanography (La Jolla, CA) and the cost of each naming:

- Nudibranch from southern Australia: $15,000

- Rare Oasisia hydrothermal vent worm from south of Easter Island, collected by the submersible Alvin; possibly the last large hydrothermal vent new species in the East Pacific: $50,000

- Phyllochaetopterus deep sea chaetopterid worm from a whalefall at 3,000 meters deep in Monterey, CA: $10,000

- Ophryotrocha worm from La Jolla, CA: $5,000

- Dinophilus worm: $5,000

- Photonectes fish, a bioluminescent deep sea predator: $25,000

12. How About an Endowed Book Fund?

Attract new major gifts from new and current prospects alike by offering endowment gifts that make a direct impact on your mission.

Stanford University Libraries & Academic Information Resources (Stanford, CA), which operates most libraries on the Stanford campus, currently has more than 250 endowed book funds. Andrew C. Herkovic, director of communications and development, says they acquire about 100,000 physical books a year.

"Roughly a quarter of our library materials budget is derived from endowments," Herkovic says. "The practice dates back to Stanford University cofounder Jane Stanford, who left her jewelry as a bequest to the library, instructing that it be sold and the proceeds placed in endowment for library acquisitions. Endowments have been created, more or less, ever since."

He notes that because the minimum threshold for a library endowment ($25,000) is far lower than the minimum for any other endowment at Stanford, it is the least expensive way for donors to enshrine their names on campus. Stanford development staff are aware of the availability of endowed book funds, Herkovic adds, and can suggest them to potential donors as a gentle introduction to endowment-scale gifts.

"With rare exceptions, people start book endowments to support subjects they care deeply about," he says. "So our objective is to identify people who are both library-friendly and have a focused interest in some topic that generally coincides with the teaching and research programs at Stanford."

To steward endowment supporters, Herkovic says, they try — through those who select the books to purchase — to stay in touch with those donors or their families. "That sometimes has the effect of yielding both additional gifts to establish funds and creating new funds," he notes. "We also have an honorary society for donors of endowed funds and their heirs called the Jewel Society (in honor of cofounder Stanford's bequest). Members are provided with publications, invitations to library events, etc., and are generally treated as elite donors."

A $25,000 endowed book fund can purchase anywhere from one to a large number of books, depending on various

---

Establishing an Endowed Book Fund

Andrew C. Herkovic, director of communications and development for Stanford University Libraries & Academic Information Resources (Stanford, CA), explains how a typical endowed book fund is established:

After discussion and negotiation, the donor and the university sign a gift or pledge agreement that states the name of the fund, its purpose and the fact that the university reserves the right to use the fund income for other purposes as it deems appropriate. "This right is not often or lightly invoked, but it is important," he says.

Based on the subject matter, the fund's proceeds are assigned to any one of the libraries' dozens of specialist selectors, who thereafter choose materials to purchase with those funds, says Herkovic. "In most cases, those materials are permanently marked — with a custom-designed bookplate — with the name of the fund, which typically includes the name of the donor and/or that of the person honored by the fund."

---

factors, says Herkovic, including the type of material purchased and the cost of the item. "Some endowments are intended and used to help acquire big-ticket items, so they may either purchase nothing in a given year, or they may augment other funds to acquire, say, a medieval manuscript or a collection of rare materials."

Endowed book funds may also be used to purchase subscriptions, databases, ephemera, prints, film, video, archival materials, rare items, etc., depending on the fund designation and the research and teaching needs of the campus. Some funds are also worded to include preservation and conservation services on specified materials (e.g., "for the acquisition and preservation of lithographs depicting the Bay Area...").

Source: Andrew C. Herkovic, Director of Communications & Development, Stanford University Libraries & Academic Information Resources, Cecil H. Green Library, Stanford University, Stanford, CA. Phone (650) 725-1877. E-mail: acherk@stanford.edu

13. Trade Large Events for Intimate Gatherings

The annual fundraiser luncheon was an important donor acquisition vehicle, but expensive, says Michele Berard, director of funds development at Butler Hospital (Providence, RI). The event collected over $130,000 but netted only around $10,000.

So when corporate sponsorship fell in 2008, staff decided to drop the luncheon in favor of smaller cultivation events. The shift in strategy was potentially risky but paid off handsomely, with $1.2 million raised the next year.

Several factors led to the breakthrough, says Berard. The more individualized format played a role, as did a shift from general operating expenses to an endowed research fund. But leveraging the connections of board members was the key development.

"We asked them to hold gatherings in their homes and invite people they knew could help the hospital with major donations," she explains. "Some were hesitant, but we told them that all they had to provide was their friends — the development office would do the rest."

Accordingly, staff assembled packets of prospective donor information, ensured that doctors and administrators attended meetings to answer questions and concerns, and even produced a 12-minute video featuring hospital research projects.

Perhaps most labor-intensive is the follow-up work staff does with contacts. No direct solicitation is made at the events, says Berard. Instead, the video presentation ends with a general appeal, and not until later are contacts called to discuss specific commitments.

Seven cultivation events have been held since the summer of 2009, resulting in gifts ranging from $1,000 to $20,000, with one outstanding contribution of $100,000. And significantly, the $1 million-plus already raised has come from just 70 gifts.

Source: Michele Berard, Director of Funds Development, Butler Hospital, Providence, RI. Phone (401) 455-6581.
E-mail: mrberard@butler.org

14. Hospital Invites Donors to Sponsor Rooms

Mercy Medical Center Foundation (Cedar Rapids, IA) is inviting donors to sponsor a patient room or other areas on one of Mercy Medical Center's floors as part of its plan to convert all its hospital rooms to private single patient rooms. Donors can also sponsor the purchase of artwork.

In recognition of the person's sponsorship, an engraved plaque is affixed on the wall outside each room or suite, or beside the sponsored artwork. The plaque contains the name of the donor(s) or the name of the person(s) they wish to memorialize with their gift. Donors are also listed in the foundation's annual report.

Since the campaign began, more than 100 of the hospital's 230 rooms have been sponsored, and they have raised a total of $500,000.

"Our room sponsorship campaign is a wonderful way for family and friends of patients to honor or memorialize a loved one or friend," says Sue Hawn, president. "It's also an opportunity for a donor to honor a physician or a member of the Mercy staff."

The campaign has been promoted primarily through direct mail, she says. A new direct mail piece was mailed at the end of July. Each direct mail piece includes a reply card and envelope. The cover letter is signed by Hawn and the chair of the foundation board.

"We also personalize some of the letters in the mailing, adding a note when we know that this opportunity to give might be of particular interest to the donor," she says. "The notes might say, 'Here's the information we talked about. I hope you'll find it to be an interesting opportunity.' Or, if one of their family members passed away, we would write a note saying that we thought they might be interested in sponsoring a room to memorialize 'X'."

> *"With the focus of this project, we have the opportunity to reach out to donors who like to make gifts in honor or memory of loved ones, nurses or physicians," says Hawn. "It is a very visible project and offers a tangible way to give."*

Hawn says they also have a general giving brochure that includes information about the room sponsorship campaign.

The cost to sponsor one patient room is $5,000. A suite sponsorship is $10,000. Other sponsorship opportunities include $1,000 for original corridor art, and $2,000 for crucifixes for the entire floor. Donors can also sponsor a nurses' station or a family waiting area for $10,000. An entire floor sponsorship is $1 million.

"With the focus of this project, we have the opportunity to reach out to donors who like to make gifts in honor or memory of loved ones, nurses or physicians," she says. "It is a very visible project and offers a tangible way to give. Many of our room sponsors come in to see their rooms."

Source: Sue Hawn, President, Mercy Medical Center Foundation, Cedar Rapids, IA. Phone (319) 398-6278.
E-mail: shawn@mercycare.org

15. Estate Gift Predictive Model Increases Efficiency, Allows Age-targeted Marketing

Frank Robertson, director of planned giving at the University of Minnesota Foundation (Minneapolis, MN), can trace the birth of the foundation's estate gift predictive model to a single incident:

"A single woman, never married and no heirs, made small annual gifts for decades, but was never identified as a major gift prospect and was never personally contacted. No one knew this woman, but she ended up leaving the university more than $3 million. The potential lost in that relationship was what really prompted us to start looking for a more reliable way of identifying potential estate donors."

The predictive model developed by foundation staff uses factors common to many estate gift donors to rate a prospect's likelihood of leaving a gift to the university (e.g., consistency of annual giving, lack of children, marital status).

Robertson says the approach has allowed the foundation to more effectively identify potential donors while extending fundraising efforts to younger demographics without wasting resources. He offers two examples of how the model has facilitated a focus on younger prospects:

1. **Targeted newsletters.** The foundation maintains two versions of a fundraising newsletter. The younger version had been targeted at donors aged 55 to 64 (the older is 65-plus). With the estate gift predictive model, though, the floor was dropped to 40 and distribution was limited to likely donors. The result, Robertson says, was fewer copies being sent, but more people likely to give being reached, and at an earlier point in life.

2. **Will survey** (shown at right). Collegiate units of the university send periodic surveys (see below) seeking confirmation of estate gift commitments to the university. The first year the foundation dropped the minimum age of recipient from 65 to 40 and contacted only the top two designations of the predictive model (the very likely and likely to give categories), they posted a 4.1 percent response rate and received seven new estate commitments from donors under age 65.

Source: Frank Robertson, Director of Planned Giving, University of Minnesota Foundation, McNamara Alumni Center, Minneapolis, MN. Phone (612) 625-0893. E-mail: Rober038@umn.edu

Will Surveys Plant Ideas, Document Decisions

Research shows that once people include a charity in their will, they rarely take it out, especially if their gift is properly stewarded, says Frank Robertson, director of planned giving at the University of Minnesota Foundation (Minneapolis, MN).

To reach potential donors and foster a culture of planned estate giving, staff use a version of the generic will survey shown below.

Sent to prospects identified by the foundation's estate gift predictive model, the survey documents gift commitments already made, which allows new donors to be incorporated into the stewardship process. It also provides a natural way to introduce potential donors to the idea of establishing an estate gift of their own.

Content not available in this edition

16. Blueprint for a Half-million-dollar Fundraiser

The Spring For Schools Luncheon of the Bellevue Schools Foundation (Bellevue, WA) draws more than 1,000 guests and raises more than $500,000 each year. Marian McDermott, manager of institutional giving, shares elements central to the event's success:

✓ **Guests in the door.** "Our priority is getting guests in the door, so we don't sell tickets," McDermott says. Rather, a volunteer-run audience development committee recruits a body of table captains who, in turn, recruit the event's many attendees.

✓ **Corporate sponsorship.** In 2010, corporate sponsorship accounted for about a fifth ($117,000) of all funds raised at the luncheon. Bellevue benefits from major area corporations like Microsoft and Boeing, but McDermott says smaller businesses are major sponsors as well. "We actively recruit board members from the business community to stay as closely connected as we can," she says. "We are always making the case that good schools produce good employees and help attract good recruits from across the country and around the world."

✓ **Targeted giving campaigns.** The event's general fundraising efforts are bolstered by two targeted giving campaigns: The Angels matching campaign invites major donors to contribute $10,000 to a fund that matches gifts up to $1,000, while the Head of the Class campaign invites prominent community members — many of them high-profile business leaders — to pledge leadership gifts ($1,000-plus) in advance of the event. These gifts, recognized in the luncheon program, provide a powerful example for others to follow, says McDermott.

✓ **Coordinated ask.** Each year, the luncheon includes a suggested specific donation for guests. The most recent suggestion was $200 per guest. This amount is communicated to guests by the table captains, all of whom receive thorough training and preparation six weeks prior to the event (see illustration).

Source: Marian McDermott, Manager of Institutional Giving, Bellevue Schools Foundation, Bellevue, WA. Phone (425) 456-4199. E-mail: Marian@bsfdn.org

The success of the Spring For Schools Luncheon of the Bellevue Schools Foundation (Bellevue, WA) depends in large part on a small army of table captains. Foundation development staff carefully coach table captains to help them succeed using tools such as this handout.

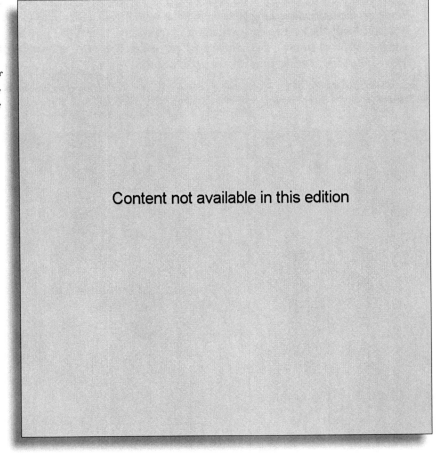

Content not available in this edition

17. ## Major Donor Club Helps University Raise Major Gifts

The University of Tennessee (UT) (Knoxville, TN) Development Council consists of approximately 70 major donors, each of whom has contributed more than $100,000 to a UT department or unit.

"Development council members are interested in being more engaged with the university and want to interact with administration at the presidential and board-of-trustee level," says Suzy Garner, director of development. "They are generous, passionate about UT (specifically those areas which they support), and want to be advocates."

Each member makes an annual gift of $1,000 to fund the council's meeting activities and the annual awards dinner, where UT's highest awards are presented, including the Development Council Service Award, the Philanthropist(s) of the Year Award and Haslam Presidential Medal.

The group meets formally twice a year. Between meetings, members participate in various activities, such as touring campus facilities made possible with private donations, interacting with faculty and students, assisting with solicitations of other alumni or friends, talking with their state representatives who direct funds to UT, hosting regional campaign events and making recommendations regarding potential prospects.

New members are recruited through current members' recommendations. Development staff is asked to make formal nominations. Garner says that most members live in Tennessee because that is where UT's highest concentration of donors are, but they encourage participation from across the country.

To keep members engaged and participating in the council, Garner says, they work hard to respond to members' feedback — whether that is making changes to meeting schedules or program content. "Many of our members go on to serve UT in other ways, such as on the UT Foundation Board and the Board of Trustees. We want them to feel like insiders and encourage as much presidential and trustee interaction as possible. Also, we try not to take up so much of their time that they can't continue to help those areas at UT about which they are most passionate."

Source: Suzy Garner, Director of Development, The University of Tennessee, Knoxville, TN. Phone (865) 974-2115.
E-mail: suzy.garner@tennessee.edu

18. ## Challenge Gift Encourages Alumni Giving

To help build a culture of annual giving at Worcester Polytechnic Institute (WPI), Worcester, MA, trustee and alumnus Mike Dolan is challenging alumni to support the institute by offering to match their $100-plus annual fund gifts, 50 cents on the dollar.

"I have a sense of obligation to pay back to the next generation what was so generously given to me," says Dolan, a chemical engineering major from WPI's class of 1975. "When I was a WPI student, there were people 20 or 30 years ahead of me who made contributions to build the buildings and hire the faculty that make WPI such a great place to learn."

The Dolan Challenge, which ran July 1, 2009, to June 30, 2010, was open to the 8,300 alumni from the classes of 1990-2009 who gave $100 or more. Three hundred eighty-three eligible alumni made donations totaling $61,500, resulting in $30,750 in matching funds. The average gift was $185.

"This represents an eight percent increase in the average gift when fiscal year 2010 is compared to fiscal year 2009. Moreover, our retention rate increased six percent between fiscal year 2008 and fiscal year 2010 (45 percent to 51 percent)," says Judith Jaeger, director of development communi-cations.

In fall 2009, all 8,300 eligible alumni received a mailing about the challenge, says Jaeger. Of those alumni, 4,615 also received a call from WPI's student calling center and/or a personal visit from an annual fund staff member, she says. "These are people who meet a variety of criteria — generally they didn't respond to the mailings, we have their permission to call them, they may have given in the past but not the previous year, etc."

WPI development staff also sent several e-mails from their annual fund board chair at the end of the calendar year to promote end-of-year giving (for tax purposes) and the Dolan Challenge to those eligible for the match.

Inserts promoting the challenge were included in all mailings to challenge-eligible alumni, says Jaeger, who notes that those who participate receive a special acknowledgement letter from Dolan.

Source: Judith Jaeger, Director of Development Communications, Office of Development and Alumni Relations, Worcester Polytechnic Institute, Worcester, MA. Phone (508) 831-5962.
E-mail: jjaeger@wpi.edu

19. Make Your Giving Societies Distinctive

Giving societies are a time-honored method of specialty stewardship — a great way to honor top donors by making them feel special. In a down economy, when major gifts are difficult to come by, it is even more important to make your giving societies stand out. But how? Comparatively, the most successful fundraising organizations share this piece of advice above all — donors who commit to certain levels of giving want to know that their contribution is making a difference. Your giving society should:

1. Grant the donor exclusive access to information and events within the organization.

2. Connect the donor to the change he/she is affecting within your organization on a personal level.

3. Work on three levels: to attract new donors, to steward donors who already have a connection to your organization, and to encourage existing donors to give at higher levels.

To achieve the three key goals, listed above, your giving society should:

❑ **Host events specifically to recognize advancements made via donations.** For instance, host a scholarship ceremony that pairs each scholarship recipient with a giving club member the recipient can mention in his/her speech and thank in person, allowing giving club members to literally put a face with their gift.

❑ **Send editorial clippings about advancements at your organization.**

❑ **Provide tours of your facility where giving club members can see their generosity at work.** The more they give, the more VIP treatment they receive. Lower-level donors might go on a group tour while higher-level donors go on individual tours with high-ranking members of your organization's leadership.

❑ **Feature donors in media presentations about your organization.**

❑ **Get creative with the breakdown of your giving club levels.** Focus less on the dollar amount and more on the giving club's community. For instance:

- A Heritage Society can recognize individuals who remember your organization in wills or insurance policies.

- An Emerging Donors giving club can honor younger donors.

- A Lifetime Club encourages long-term, sustained giving.

❑ **Personalize.** Even in a big institution, each member of a giving club needs to feel exclusive and special. To achieve this:

- Write correspondence by hand, whenever reasonable.

- Supplement business calls with personal touches, for instance call on the donor's anniversary of membership.

- Give out color-coded tickets to events. You know that not everyone can be invited to all events, but the donor receiving the events package will get the feeling of being part of something elite.

Gift Ideas to Tell Your Top Donors 'Thanks'

Looking to thank your giving clubs' top donors for their support? Consider:

✓ Commemorative certificates and lapel pins so they can proudly display evidence of their commitment to you.

✓ A plaque or engraved gift presented to major giving club donors by a direct recipient/beneficiary of their gifts.

✓ Gifts donated by community members — magazine subscriptions, coupons, gift certificates — which represent no cost to your organization, but make donors feel like they are getting star treatment.

Sources: Marie J. Maher, Director of Development and Alumni Relations, University of Minnesota, Rochester, MN. Phone (507) 258-8059. E-mail: mmaher@umn.edu
Keri Muuss, Director of Communication and Donor Relations, The Children's Hospital Foundation, Aurora, CO.
Phone (720) 777-1765 E-mail: kmuuss@tchfden.org.
Website: www.thechildrenshospitalfoundation.org

20. Solicit Major Gifts Through Your Website

To spur online giving, Carnegie Mellon University (Pittsburgh, PA) launched an online giving site in conjunction with its $1 billion Inspire Innovation Campaign.

Jay Brown, director of marketing for Web communications, says online giving has gone up 3 percent since they tied the website to the campaign.

Brown says, the university received an average of 245 gifts a month during the fiscal year, with total monthly giving averaging $58,261. Most donors were alumni, with 26 percent of online donors directing their gift to the unrestricted Carnegie Mellon Fund.

The university's simplified, user-friendly online giving form (www.cmu.edu/campaign/ways/online.html) consists of three steps: About You, Your Gift and Payment. After completing each section, the donor clicks "Next" to move to the next page. Buttons throughout the university's website show users where they should click to give.

"We also keep looking for opportunities to drive more traffic to the site," Brown says, "such as advertising our online giving option in our quarterly magazine and adding a short link in every direct mail piece that connects people to the online form."

Online donors receive an automatically generated receipt and receive phone solicitations and other stewardship based on their giving level.

Source: Jay Brown, Director of Marketing for Web Communications, Carnegie Mellon University, Pittsburgh, PA. Phone (412) 268-1913. E-mail: jsbrown@andrew.cmu.edu

21. Tours Get Major Donors Passionate About Your Cause

Development staff with The Clinic (Phoenixville, PA), a medical clinic for the uninsured, began offering donor prospects tours in February 2009 to get them engaged and passionate about supporting the clinic's mission.

The 30-minute clinic tours are conducted near the end of business day, between 3:30 and 4 p.m., and led by Debbie Shupp, development director, or Krys Sipple, the clinic's executive director.

Tours end in Sipple's office, with the opportunity for the participants to chat with a board member and ask any questions.

> *"Involvement in the tours makes our board members feel good... They are not expected to ask for money, just to tell their story."*

"Involvement in the tours makes our board members feel good," says Shupp. "I've never had a board member say they won't do it. They are not expected to ask for money, just to tell their story."

About 60 percent of the board has participated in the tours, and the rest just haven't had an opportunity yet, she says: "We've only held about two dozen tours so far."

At the end of each tour, participants are given brochures, newsletters and sometimes event invitations, thanked and invited to come back.

Shupp recruits tour participants when out networking at organizations, churches, clubs and the Chamber of Commerce. "I always give out my card and ask if they are interested in coming in for a tour," she says.

She also recruits tour participants by tracking consistent donors. "I do this by looking at gifts that reflect the donor's care for the clinic," she says. "I call them to thank them for their gift and ask if they've been here. If not, I ask them to come in for a tour."

Once someone is brought in for a tour, he or she is always on board, says Shupp: "We've had donors say 'You painted the walls?' or 'Wow, I didn't expect you to have done this or that.' When they do, I always ask, 'What were you expecting?' The donor might say, 'Cold, cement walls.' And I will reply, 'We have great volunteers here who have worked to paint all the rooms and keep everything nice.'"

Shupp follows up after the tour with an e-mail thank-you. She also adds the tour participants to the clinic's mailing list.

The tours have been very successful in attracting donors, she says: "Seventy-five percent of those who go on the tours end up making a donation. Donations range from $50 to several thousand dollars."

In addition to attracting donations, the tours have also been great at building relationships, says Shupp. For example, she says, one tour participant from a local church asked to be an outreach partner for the clinic, and another asked to help with the clinic's wish list.

Source: Debbie Shupp, Development Director, The Clinic, Phoenixville, PA. Phone (610) 935-1134, ext. 24. E-mail: dshupp@theclinicpa.org

22. Student-driven Event Raises $1 Million Over Five Years

Since 2004, National Honor Society high school students from Northport High (Northport, NY) have planned and organized A Midwinter Night's Dream — a special event that raises funds for Amyotrophic Lateral Sclerosis (ALS) research.

Their peers established the event five years ago after their beloved teacher, David Deutsch, was diagnosed with ALS, also known as Lou Gehrig's Disease. They initially organized a three-on-three basketball tournament and raised $32,000 for ALS research. After attending a major ALS fundraiser in New York City, the students decided they wanted to do more. The first annual event, A Midwinter Night's Dream, raised $90,000.

Held each January, the 2009 event drew 550 guests to Oheka Castle on Long Island and raised $345,000, bringing the five-year fundraising total to $1,067,000. In addition, in June 2009 they opened their own research lab, entitled A Midwinter Night's Dream Cryopreservation Lab, at Stony Brook University Medical Center (Stony Brook, NY).

Throughout the year, the students are responsible for contacting large and small companies to ask for sponsorships to the event. The companies then appear in the commemorative journal given to all event guests.

Event tickets are $150 per person and raffle tickets (winner gets to choose one of three vacations) generate significant funds. The gala features live entertainment, dinner, a student-run presentation, and silent and live auctions.

"Our organization is motivated completely by the local ALS patients we visit monthly," says Don Strasser, executive director of A Midwinter Night's Dream. "It's important that the students see who we are fighting for.... It not only inspires the students to continue to fight against ALS, but also gives hope to the patients and their families. In addition to this, we also send students to prestigious research centers over the summer to observe and conduct ALS research. This gives the students the opportunity to see where the money we raise goes and how much the research facilities need it."

Source: Don Strasser, Executive Director, A Midwinter Night's Dream, Northport High School National Honor Society, Northport, NY. Phone (631) 262-7428. E-mail: dstrasser9@optonline.net. Website: www.amnd.org

---

Tips to Maximize Student-driven Success

For five years, Don Strasser has successfully managed students at Northport High School National Honor Society (Northport, NY) as they raised funds for ALS research through the popular event, a Midwinter Night's Dream. Strasser shares tips for managing a young group of event organizers:

- **Treat it like a job.** "Students are chosen for our organization based on an application and interview process, much like applying for a job. This narrows a large group of students down to a smaller, more motivated group of about 40 willing to do extra work to get things done. It also teaches students to work hard for something they want instead of just handing it to them (and) proves to the advisors that these students will make a positive impact on the organization because they have the will to work more than others."

- **Encourage communication.** "We e-mail each other constantly about tasks that need to be completed, important events, good news, etc. Without good communication and monthly meetings, we are unable to work together as a successful team."

- **Connect them to the cause.** "Students work so much better if they have a reason to. Teach them about the cause, introduce them to inspirational people and get them excited about what they have ahead. If there is no connection to the cause, the fundraising will be harder and not as successful."

- **Give them individual goals.** "Each year, we give the students personal goals they are encouraged to complete by the event. For example, each committee member is asked to raise $5,000 for A Midwinter Night's Dream as a personal fundraising goal. They are also asked to sell a certain number of raffle tickets.... They motivate each other to get their jobs done."

- **Keep them in the loop.** "If you keep them updated on important developments and news within the organization, they become more motivated and excited about their jobs. For example, we keep the students updated about how much money we have raised so far this year so they know what needs to be done to complete the year's goal."

23. Partner With Chamber of Commerce to Reach Businesses

In 2009, the Issaquah Schools Foundation (Issaquah, WA) entered into a fundraising/awareness-raising partnership with the local chamber of commerce that raises money while uniting the community around the common cause of education, says Robin Callahan, executive director of the Issaquah Schools Foundation. Callahan answers questions about the partnership:

How did the partnership come about?

"We received feedback about our previous business partnership campaign that the entry point for recognition, $1,500, was too much for local businesses. They wanted to commit, but couldn't always afford that kind of gift. So we began talking to our chamber of commerce about how the vitality of our community is dependent on the success of our schools. Together, we thought of ways the chamber could raise awareness about community involvement strengthening the district."

How does the program work?

"Local businesses can contribute at different levels, for different levels of recognition, which they choose from a menu of support (see below). The lowest level, $50 gift, gives you a cling sticker for the window of your business, touting your business as a 'Business Partner — Proud to Invest in Great Schools and Great Communities.' It goes up from there."

How do you advertise your program?

"It happened that a local periodical had an entire issue of the magazine about how great schools make great communities, including a piece from the Executive Director of the Chamber, another from the Superintendent of Schools, and how it is that strong schools promote vital and healthy community. So that summer, I sat down to write a letter with the chamber to be sent to all business members of the chamber, and we called upon that information to raise awareness for the foundation."

Source: Robin Callahan, Executive Director, Issaquah Schools Foundation, Issaquah, WA. Phone (425) 416-2045. E-mail: rcallahan@issaquahschoolsfoundation.org. Website: www.issaquahschoolsfoundation.org

Partnership Raises Funds, Awareness

A year-old partnership with the local chamber of commerce is beginning to pay off for the Issaquah Schools Foundation (Issaquah, WA), says Robin Callahan, the foundation's executive director:

"We've raised $2,500 to date, which covers our cost, but the initial benefit is that we've raised our participation level significantly: 40 businesses have responded (out of 400), which is 40 new business partners that we didn't have before.

"The feedback we've been getting has been positive; business owners say they appreciate being able to support their schools, they didn't know the foundation was out there, and they didn't know there was a need. This is the most promising element: We are spreading our message. We will be doing it again next year."

Content not available in this edition

White Coat Day Gets to the Heart of Fundraising

The Holy Cross Hospital Foundation (Taos, NM) has found a unique way to treat heart conditions while also raising funds and building ties.

"Relationships are the heart of fundraising," says Sally Trigg, executive director. To nurture relationships, the foundation presents White Coat Day, an invitation-only, inside view of the people and programs at the heart of the hospital.

Every month, approximately 30 people are invited to participate in White Coat Day. The invitation goes to donors, governmental leaders, media people, business owners and interested community members.

Attendees have lunch, hear some stories from doctors and tour an area of the hospital. Trigg says the attendees receive special treatment while on the tour, wearing white coats emblazoned with VIP buttons. Participants also learn about new hospital programs, plans for the future and important current health care concerns.

Trigg says the benefits of the program are innumerable.

"It helps the participants learn about the hospital in a relaxed, enjoyable atmosphere, instead of when they are sick or anxious as a patient or a visitor. They also meet hospital staff and doctors and learn more about them and the other participants. It helps the foundation because more people learn about the hospital and about the focuses of our fundraising. It helps the community by increasing knowledge — attendees pass on the word about programs and services that are available — and it creates bridges," she says.

Source: Sally Trigg, Executive Director, Holy Cross Hospital Foundation, Taos, NM. Phone (575) 751-5811. E-mail: strigg@taoshospital.org. Website: www.taoshospital.org

 ## Award Encourages Faculty Fundraising

The University of Arizona Foundation (Tucson, AZ) developed the Eugene G. Sander Endowed Faculty Fundraising Award in 2008 to encourage faculty members to become involved in fundraising.

The award honors Eugene G. Sander, dean of the College of Agriculture and Life Sciences, who founded and for 21 years chaired, the Deans Plus Development Committee, which encouraged active fundraising involvement at college and department levels.

Sander has helped raise tens of millions of dollars in private contributions, says John C. Brown, director of communication and marketing.

The award acknowledges University of Arizona (UA) faculty members who demonstrate extraordinary leadership in fundraising that benefits university programs. Nominations are sought from the entire university community between July 1 and October 1 for faculty who played an instrumental role in development during the previous fiscal year. The selection committee includes the presidents of the University of Arizona Foundation, the provost, and the senior vice president of development and university campaigns.

Award recipients receive a certificate and a one-time payout from a UA Foundation endowment fund to be used for professional development or to support and build the fundraising program for the recipient's college or department. The foundation board of trustees presents the award to the recipient at an annual dinner and reception.

The award's first recipient was Soyeon Shim, director of the School of Family and Consumer Sciences. Shim received the honor in 2008 for spearheading a $25 million fundraising campaign to build the new McClelland Park building to house the John and Doris Norton School of Family and Consumer Sciences.

The 2009 award recipient was John W. Olsen, regent's professor in anthropology and former department chair of the School of Anthropology. Olsen, the JE Tsongkapa Chair in Anthropology, raised more than $18 million in the last five years for the school and increased giving to the College of Social and Behavioral Sciences from $800,000 to $5 million a year. In the 2007-'08 academic year, Olsen secured an $8 million gift for UA — the largest single gift the college has ever received from a private donor.

"The Faculty Fundraising Award reinforces to faculty that part of their job is to fundraise," says Brown. "This emphasis on development starts with the president and provost who place a high value on development work at this institution, as evidenced by their institutional endowment of this annual award."

The UA Foundation Board of Trustees endowed the award.

Brown says hopes are for the award to help grow a more visible culture of philanthropy among faculty on campus: "Some faculty might feel uncomfortable asking for money, but they now see it as finding partners. Donors are inspired and feel rewarded by helping to transform a department's research and teaching."

News about award recipients is publicized in the UA Foundation's magazine; on the University's official news outlet, UANews.org; and in an ad in the student newspaper in the last issue of the semester, which is the university's congratulatory issue.

Source: John C. Brown, Director, Communication & Marketing, The University of Arizona Foundation, Tucson, AZ. Phone (520) 621-5581. E-mail: brown@al.arizona.edu

26. Giving Program Lets Employees Direct How Funds Are Used

Every year, the staff at Saint Patrick Hospital (Missoula, MT) donate more than $100,000 to their hospital's Health Foundation.

Donations come via their 30 Minute Club, a giving program that allows employees to donate 30 minutes worth of pay from each bimonthly paycheck and direct the money toward hospital programs of their choosing.

Kathryn McCleerey, health foundation annual campaign development officer, says that the 30 Minute Club (nicknamed 30 MC) is a long-standing part of the Spirit of Giving campaign that helps employees support the hospital in ways most meaningful to them.

McCleerey explains how the 30 MC giving program works:

✓ Employees choose the amount they wish to donate per paycheck: either 30 minutes worth of pay or another specified amount.

✓ Employees then select from more than 30 programs to support, from cardiology to cancer, scholarship funds to patient support groups.

✓ Every dollar that the employee sacrifices from his/her paycheck goes directly into the fund that he/she has selected, with nothing taken out for expenses.

Because the giving program deals with an internal group of donors, McCleery says, it is low-cost and low-maintenance. It is a part-time job for a single employee to promote and serve as the program's point person. Promotional activities are low-cost because they can occur during established events, such as new employee orientation and the employee benefits fair.

Additionally, she says, the program is designed to be self-sufficient: Using the hospital website and employee intranet, employees may sign up, change their level of participation, and change the program they wish to support. The foundation then communicates with human resources to let them know the amount to deduct each paycheck, as the employee has directed, McCleerey says, noting, "Employees appreciate that response time is almost immediate when any change is requested."

McCleerey says more than 30 percent of employees participate in the program. The foundation hosts an annual thank-you luncheon or breakfast for the participants.

Beyond that, she says, the program is its own reward. "[Participants] know that 100 percent of their contribution is being directed to the programs they care most deeply about. Within our gentle culture, we do not directly solicit employees for the program — it is appropriate for us to simply promote and inform."

Source: Kathryn L. McCleerey, Development Officer, St. Patrick Hospital and Health Foundation, Missoula, MT. Phone (406) 327-3052.
E-mail: kmccleerey@saintpatrick.org.
Website: www.stpatsfoundation.org

Content not available in this edition

Content not available in this edition

27. Dream Vacation Homes Raise Funds for Nonprofits

Vacation Homes for Charity (VH4C) of Lakewood, CO, enables homeowners to put unused time at a vacation home to good use while supporting nonprofits.

Homeowners complete an application at www.vacationhomesforcharity.org, showing the number of nights available at their vacation home and the value placed on that designated time. The donation is matched to the nonprofit or charity the donor designates on the application.

The use of the vacation home is then put up for live auction, raffle or silent auction to generate funds for a nonprofit.

Nonprofits complete charity profiles at www.vacationhomesforcharity.org. Staff from VH4C contact the nonprofit to offer them donation options that meet their criteria.

Michael McFadden, VH4C co-founder, answers questions on the process:

How do you reach persons willing to donate time at their vacation homes?

"Our company, The Society of Leisure Enthusiasts, works with owners and managers of luxury vacation rentals promoting the idea of donating to all clients and prospects. Our mantra is 'Do Good with Vacation Homes.' We're also members of Vacation Rental Managers Association and promote VH4C through them. Most owners, managers and resorts like to use our service because we create all the marketing materials and work directly with the charities. Charities like working with us because they can source several vacations with one call."

How many vacation homes were rented in 2009 to raise funds and how much was raised in 2009?

"We participated in 61 events and helped raise $216,000 for charities."

How much was donated directly to charities in 2009?

"Approximately $148,000 went directly to the charities. The remaining amount was used to cover cleaning costs and fees. More than 60 participating nonprofits are listed at the organization's website — all have benefited from the vacation home donation process. In 2010, VH4C expects to double its efforts in fundraising."

Source: Michael McFadden, Co-Founder, Vacation Homes for Charity — The Society of Leisure Enthusiasts, Lakewood, CO. Phone (866) 789-8222. E-mail: mike@thesociety.com. Website: www.vacationhomesforcharity.org

28. Younger Board Members Can Boost Fundraising

A board of trustees is typically a gathering place for baby boomers. Shake things up by involving younger people to draw on their energy and innovation.

Kiernan Doherty is president of Levé (Portland, OR), a nonprofit that supports other charities through fundraising, volunteering and other outreach efforts — and whose board members are all under age 29.

Levé selects one charity a year to focus on, a project that often includes Levé members serving on those charities' ambassador boards — junior boards specifically tasked with producing special events that will attract young donors.

Here are three ways Levé board members have worked with other nonprofits:

❑ Since joining the ambassador board of Friends of the Children-Portland (Portland, OR) mentoring service three years ago, Levé's secretary, Maddie O'Neill, has planned and executed annual bowl-a-thons for the organization that have raised $290,000 to date. The bowl-a-thon has become the Friends of the Children's signature event for young adults, while its renowned charity auction still targets an older, more affluent crowd.

❑ Past Levé president Courtney Francis served on the ambassador board of YWCA Yolanda House (Portland, OR) in 2006. That year the board organized the first-ever YWCA Off Key, now a regular karaoke fundraiser, that brought in more than $20,000. The partnership helped the YWCA activate a new and younger donor base while increasing exposure among a younger demographic.

❑ Francis created a signature fundraiser for Saturday Academy (Portland, OR), which provides academic enrichment opportunities for underprivileged children. The event, BrainGames trivia night, has generated 160 new, unique donors to Saturday Academy and increased its exposure tenfold to a new audience and demographic.

Source: Kiernan Doherty, President, Levé, Portland, OR. Phone (503) 320-7076. E-mail: kdoherty@metgroup.com. Website: www.leve-nw.org

29. Put 'Friendraising' Before Fundraising When Building Program From the Ground Up

With proper planning, execution and leadership, even a first-time major fundraising effort can be an overwhelming success.

When Janice Y. Benjamin became vice president of development for The University of Kansas Hospital (Kansas City, KS) in 2001, the hospital had never had its own formal fundraising program, and had approximately $500,000 in available funds, all raised by the Kansas University (KU) Endowment Association, the fundraising arm of the University of Kansas.

According to Benjamin, the hospital became an independently governed state authority in 1998, which allowed it to compete in the marketplace and focus on a core strategy — putting patients first. Although the hospital was still part of the academic medical center, she says it needed to have its own identity in the community, noting that to be successful in fundraising, an organization must build a constituency of advocates, and put "friend raising before fundraising."

She started with an internal and external assessment, bringing in a fundraising consultant to conduct a feasibility study. "The consultant's summary said that we would be lucky to raise $1 million in five years," she says. "We ended up raising $1 million in our first full year of fundraising. Our success confirmed that the hospital should be proactive in developing a fundraising program; there was obviously a lot of untapped potential."

"Once we were able to build an identity, show some success and report outcomes, it was much easier to attract philanthropy," says Benjamin. "I believe that people want to give to winners to help them become even more successful. If you can prove that you are doing things right — which in our case, is providing advanced, compassionate care — people will want to support you."

While maintaining a strong partnership with each other, the hospital's development program separated from the KU Endowment Association and opened its own Office of Fund Development. All gifts to the hospital are still processed through the KU Endowment Association, which also manages and invests the hospital's funds.

To work within Health Insurance Portability and Accountability Act (HIPAA) regulations, which protect patient information, Benjamin and staff created a letter template that physicians can use to make the initial contact with a patient-donor prospect. When a physician identifies a grateful patient, the physician's assistant sends the letter, which invites the patient to learn more about a particular program's philanthropic needs. The director of development follows up and keeps the physician involved.

"When cultivating and stewarding major donors, you have to think about how to make it a unique experience for them," Benjamin says. "We use shadowing — allowing a donor to come in, visit with a physician and watch a procedure being performed; one-on-one lunch meetings with the CEO; and the opportunity for donors to share their advice by serving on an advisory council."

They also use prospect research tools such as those offered by WealthEngine (Bethesda, MD) as a systematized way to identify patients with capacity, Benjamin says. To reach out to these persons, "we establish a series of 'touches,' which can include a hospital visit from the development staff or leadership with a small gift and letter sent a few weeks after discharge with our newsletter, Good Medicine. This newsletter contains stories about hospital initiatives that demonstrate the impact of philanthropy from grateful patients."

While moving the hospital from one with no formal fundraising program to one with a highly successful program has been an inspirational challenge, Benjamin says it was one reason she took the job: "You definitely have to think about what motivates you. You also need to surround yourself with people who are resourceful and understand that you must spend money to make money and attract the right volunteer base."

Source: Janice Y. Benjamin, Vice President of Development, The University of Kansas Hospital, Westwood, KS. Phone (913) 588-1435. E-mail: jbenjamin2@kumc.edu

Steps to Multi-million-dollar Fundraising Success

Janice Y. Benjamin, vice president of development, The University of Kansas Hospital (Kansas City, KS), shares the top three strategies that she believes helped to build a fundraising program that has raised $37 million in its first seven years:

1. **Win over the internal staff.** To help the hospital's physicians and nurses recognize the value of philanthropy, Benjamin asked physicians to donate funds to start a recognition program for nurses. Nurses are nominated for the awards by their peers, and a committee chooses the winners. The awards are presented during an annual awards ceremony.

2. **Develop a successful annual event.** The hospital staff partnered with Kansas Speedway for an annual event to benefit the hospital's cancer patients. Helping the hospital raise more than $3.3 million in seven years, Treads & Threads was not only a way to gain immediate visibility among companies, she says, it has become their signature event and one of the top 10 events in Kansas City. The last event attracted 107 corporate sponsors. They also created a brand for corporate sponsorships called Companies Committed to Care.

3. **Concentrate on major gifts.** Major donor prospects are primarily identified through the hospital's Grateful Patient Program. "Our physicians and nurses help us identify families with an interest in giving to the hospital," she says. "Most gifts are a result of the patients' and their families' relationships with their care teams."

30. Christmas Card List Can Be Gift to Fundraising Campaign

Get creative to come up with new ideas for reaching out with your campaign and fundraising materials.

Courtney Day, past executive director of the Up 'til Dawn letter-writing campaign fundraiser at California State University (Long Beach, CA), says they urged students participating in the effort "to hit their parents up for their Christmas card list."

Day cites three reasons why having students write to persons on these lists has helped boost the campaign, which since 2005 has generated more than $100,000 for its beneficiary, St. Jude Children's Research Hospital (Memphis, TN):

❑ Generally the people on those lists are older and more accomplished in their chosen careers and lifestyles, thus in a better position to give.

❑ The personal connection between the student writer and the addressee also helps increase the likelihood of a gift.

❑ The lists are usually up-to-date with accurate spelling of names and contact info.

Source: Courtney Day, past Executive Director, Up 'til Dawn, California State University at Long Beach, Long Beach, CA. Phone (562) 243-2069. E-mail: courtneymday@gmail.com

31. Cruise Fundraiser Offers Chance to Build Camaraderie

What would you say to raising more than $5,000 with minimal effort while providing a camaraderie-building opportunity for volunteers and members?

"Easy money" is the term used by Ellen Krivchenia, Planned Giving and Major Gifts officer, Deborah Hospital Foundation (Brown Mills, NJ), of the cruises the foundation offers to chapter members.

"The cruises offer the opportunity for chapter members from the Northeast (New Jersey and New York) to the Southeast (Florida) to join together to support the foundation, boosting camaraderie," she says. They promote the cruise opportunities to all chapter members and anyone interested in joining the foundation's contingency.

The foundation accepts bids for the cruise from several travel agents who have worked with individual Deborah chapters in the past. The winning agent makes the arrangements with the cruise line, makes the individuals' reservations, keeps the foundation cruise chairperson informed of the status and communicates with passengers several times leading up to the cruise.

The foundation is responsible for reviewing and approving the budget and the recommended cruise line, along with creating and distributing all publicity.

Krivchenia says the cruises benefit the foundation and everyone involved:

"Our constituents pay reasonable rates and do not pay additional money for the donation to Deborah. On the cruise they are our ambassadors, speaking passionately about our organization to other passengers who do not know of our special hospital. They also have the opportunity to share successful fundraising and membership ideas with each other."

She says the cruises have been so successful that the organization's leadership has agreed to offer a second cruise in one year. The seven-day cruise sailed from Miami, FL, in December 2010, with more than 100 cabins booked. The foundation receives $50 per cabin, with all funds raised supporting patient care at Deborah Heart and Lung Center, a specialty cardiac, vascular and pulmonary medical center in Southern New Jersey, which does not bill its patients for their medical care.

Source: Ellen Krivchenia, Planned Giving and Major Gifts Officer, Deborah Hospital Foundation, Brown Mills, NJ. Phone (609) 893-3372. E-mail: ekrivchenia@deborahFoundation.org

---

Five Tips for Cruise Fundraiser Success

Ellen Krivchenia, Planned Giving and Major Gifts officer, Deborah Hospital Foundation (Brown Mills, NJ), shares five tips to help make your cruise fundraiser successful:

1. Begin advertising as soon as possible, up to 12 months before the cruise.

2. Make sure the travel agent you are working with communicates well and has follow-up with all passengers.

3. Make sure you get accurate and up-to-date records on cruisers from the travel agent.

4. Offer a small gift to your passengers including your logo, phone number and website. Just remember to take into consideration the delivery of the items to the ship and the distribution of the items to the passengers when selecting the gift item.

5. When determining the time of year to offer a cruise, take cruise price changes and severe weather conditions into consideration, both based on the time of year.

32. Grateful Patient Program Invites Thanks, Gifts

Gratitude — whether for an education, a community service, a medical procedure or other reason — is a major motivation of all philanthropic giving. This appreciation is the focus of the Memorial Medical Center Foundation's (Springfield, IL) grateful patient program.

"One of the central aims of the program is simply letting patients know that the medical center is a not-for-profit organization, and that gifts are always appreciated," says Elena Kezelis, executive director of the foundation.

Just as important, she says, is the opportunity to write a note of thanks to physicians or staff members. "People might not have returned to work or be facing insurance difficulties, and having a way to express gratitude in a non-financial way is very meaningful."

Staff distribute several thousand grateful patient brochures every year. Of those that are returned, Kezelis estimates about half include donations and half are simply messages of thanks. Donations range from $10 in cash to $10,000 in stock transfers.

The brochures are stocked in all waiting rooms, and several times a year, foundation staff send them in age- and ZIP code-targeted mailings.

Involving physicians and nurse managers in the program is also key to successfully connecting grateful patients to giving opportunities, says Kezelis.

While the effort does not always end with a check in hand, she says it provides other benefits that are vitally important in their own right, "Nursing is tough, physical work, and caregivers love to be reminded that what they do is making a difference."

Source: Elena Kezelis, Executive Director, Memorial Medical Center Foundation, Springfield, IL. Phone (217) 788-4706. E-mail: Kezelis.Elena@mhsil.com

Stocked in all waiting rooms and sent to targeted audiences, this brochure encourages words of praise and financial gifts to the Memorial Medical Center Foundation (Springfield, IL).

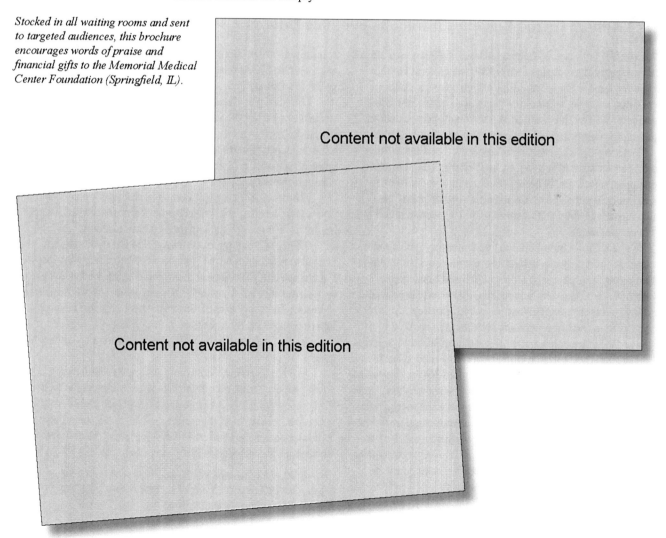

Content not available in this edition

Content not available in this edition

33. Three Ways Chapters Can Boost Fundraising Efforts

While the University of Texas Alumni Association (Austin, TX) features two full-time employees dedicated to supporting alumni chapters, the chapters themselves are run and organized fully by volunteers.

That strong commitment by volunteers helps the university reach its fundraising goals, says Nate Carty, past president of the association's New York Texas Exes chapter (New York, NY). Carty says the university benefits from this strong volunteer involvement in the following ways:

✓ Individual chapters use their profits to fund scholarships that are awarded generally to incoming students from the chapter's area. Says Carty, "For New York, where the university has made extensive efforts to recruit students, we have been able to offer incoming students scholarships of up to $2,000. In 2010, we awarded a total of $12,000 in scholarships. These scholarships further the goals of the university in recruiting, but require no effort on the part of the University directly."

✓ Local volunteers are more familiar with both the constituency of our chapter as well as the venues available for events. We have partnered with the university on several occasions to host events relating to various capital campaigns.

✓ The chapters help to keep the local alumni feeling connected to the university, no matter where they reside. The more connected the alumni feel to the school, the more receptive they will be to the fundraising efforts of the university.

Source: Nate Carty, Past President, New York Texas Exes, Astoria, NY. Phone (347) 286-8789. E-mail: ncarty@alumni.utexas.net

34. Annual Giving Societies Attract $1,000-plus Donors

Children's Healthcare of Atlanta (Atlanta, GA) has two annual leadership giving societies for $1,000-plus donors: Hope's Circle for female donors and Will's Club for male donors.

Hope's Circle, started five years ago, has nearly 250 members. Will's Club, started about a year ago with about 25 donors, has nearly tripled in size to almost 70 members.

Both are opt-in, meaning members are not automatically enrolled, but must agree to join, says Elesha Mavrommatis, development officer. "The opt-in feature helps us identify donors who want to be contacted on a regular basis," she says. "In effect, they self-identify as being open to a call from a development officer."

Hope's Circle members receive a monthly e-newsletter as well as invitations to behind-the-scenes tours, roundtable discussions with physicians, luncheons and other donor events. Will's Club members receive a quarterly e-newsletter and invitations to member-hosted events. Both groups are recognized in the organization's community report, on signage at the hospitals and on the medical facility's website.

"While Hope's Circle is staff-driven — I coordinate tours and events — Will's Club is member-driven," says Mavrommatis. "Will's Club members plan their own events and are more active recruiters for the group. For the men, it's a way to socialize with other men who want to support the hospital. I believe that long-term, the men's group will be successful because they feel ownership of it." Events organized by the men's group to date include skeet shooting, a wine tasting, a tour and tasting at a local brewery.

Mavrommatis says switching giving society membership due dates from anniversary date to calendar year has made tracking membership much easier. For example, members who give in 2009 are recognized as 2009 donors and have all of 2010 to make a qualifying gift for the next fiscal year.

The giving societies are promoted in the organization's annual fund brochure and on its website, and information about the groups are communicated to major gift officers and corporate gift officers who might have donors who would qualify as members but who may not make a gift directly through the annual fund.

When a qualifying gift comes in through the annual fund, staff send an acknowledgement that includes the opportunity to join the giving society and how to do so.

"When we call them to thank them for their gift, we will also mention it again," she says. "Once they join Hope's Circle, we call to welcome them and send them the last e-newsletter that went out, which includes my contact information sent under my e-mail address. This helps me develop a relationship with these donors."

Will's Club communicates almost exclusively through e-mail.

At Thanksgiving, Mavrommatis sends handwritten cards to all Hope's Circle members. The same happens for Will's Club members. Hope's Circle and Will's Club members also receive a holiday card by e-mail, activities she says help develop a relationship with these donors, which is an important element in the success of the giving societies.

Source: Elesha Mavrommatis, Development Officer, Children's Healthcare of Atlanta, Atlanta, GA. Phone (404) 785-7336. E-mail: Elesha.Mavrommatis@choa.org

35. Celebrate Successful Employee Campaigns

The Methodist Hospital Foundation (Indianapolis, IN) — the fundraising arm of Methodist Hospital — raised $1.8 million from 700 employees in its employee-focused campaign, Lighting the Way: The Campaign for Methodist Hospital, March 2-June 11, 2010.

Throughout all phases of the campaign, foundation officials focused on multiple creative ways to engage employees individually and as part of department teams, says Laura King, the foundation's director of marketing and communications.

Those efforts, from campaign kick-off to closing celebration, included:

❑ **Hand-picking and training a campaign cabinet.** This group came together in June 2009, with ambassadors, known as luminaries, also chosen and trained as the troops on the ground for the campaign. Throughout the campaign, cabinet members and luminaries received regular updates and tips on soliciting employees and information-sharing via weekly e-mails. In addition they were given a tool kit of materials to use for solicitations, including a case statement, artist renderings of the new tower, information on how to make asks or raise funds, a pledge envelope and Beacon Club brochure.

❑ **Implementing an internal communications strategy several months before the campaign launch,** employees were educated about philanthropy and how fundraising has supported the hospital over its 100-plus-year history.

❑ **Hosting campaign kick-off events.** Senior leaders, campaign cabinet members and luminaries served spaghetti in the cafeteria to third-shift employees in a celebration that included music and cupcakes. A daytime kickoff reception featured hospital leadership posing as paparazzi photographing employees as they walked down the carpet into the reception area. Cabinet members wore formal attire, including tuxedos for the men, says King.

❑ **Encouraging individual employee departments to develop their own fundraising initiatives.** This effort generated an idea by the Emergency Response Training Institute to resurrect the tradition of bed races. As part of the end-of-campaign celebration, employees from various departments raced against each other with makeshift hospital beds designed, decorated and built for speed. The bed races included a parade of participants, inspection of beds and voting for favorite bed designs. Teams paid $200 entrance fees.

❑ **Spotlighting the Beacon Club,** for employees who donate one hour of pay per month for three years, drew 333 members.

Organizers dressed the hospital with window treatments, banners, column wraps, hanging signs and posters representing the campaign theme. They built a glass replica of the Lighthouse of Health beacon that sits atop Methodist Hospital to use as a tote board, lighting up at various campaign milestones, which, King says, "created significant buzz throughout the campaign."

Source: Laura King, Director, Marketing & Communications, Methodist Hospital Foundation, Indianapolis, IN. Phone (317) 962-4537. E-mail: lking3@clarian.org

Content not available in this edition

Strategies Boost Employee Gifts

Laura King, director of marketing and communications, Methodist Hospital Foundation (Indianapolis, IN), shares strategies that engaged hospital employees and raised $1.8 million in its Lighting the Way employee campaign:

✓ Direct mail postcards sent at campaign start.

✓ One-on-one meetings with senior executives, directors and managers.

✓ More than 60 presentations to departments by the foundation's development staff.

✓ Pre-campaign touches dating back to summer 2009 to build awareness for the foundation and the campaign, including an ice cream social, coffee-and-donut mornings and a silent auction that raised $20,000.

✓ Reminder events such as coffee and donuts and live jazz in the main hallways and sale of specialty coffee drinks at the local café with proceeds going to the campaign.

✓ Departmental fundraisers, from bake sales, book sales, treadmill-athon and dress-down days to offers to bake and decorate cakes.

✓ A series of e-mails to employees from Methodist Hospital President Samuel L. Odle with an overview of a selected personal story and a link to the foundation's website, where video stories were posted, along with a link to the donation page with the words, "Make your donation now!".

36. Travel Programs Can Enhance Fundraising Efforts

Consider offering opportunities for your major donors to mix and mingle, for both short and extended periods, to nurture their connections to your organization and one another.

One way to do so is to offer travel opportunities. Judge interest levels and build camaraderie among this important group with day-long jaunts to choice destinations within your service region. If those prove successful, move to one- or two-night stays that include destinations and adventures that appeal to your major supporters.

Next step? A travel program that offers the opportunity to travel to desirable destinations across the country and planet.

Here, two organizations share information about their travel programs — the first of which offers travel to major donors as well as other supporters of its organization, and the second which offers travel as a benefit exclusively to major donors:

McGill University (Montreal, Quebec, Canada):

Each year, McGill University (Montreal, Quebec, Canada) offers 25 to 30 educational travel opportunities for interested alumni, parents and friends. Destinations include Antarctica, Egypt, Peru, Japan and Nepal.

"At McGill we have not looked at the travel program as a breeding ground for major gifts," says Leisha LeCouvie, director of parent and affinity programs. "That being said, some of our travelers have been very generous. There is no formal major gift solicitation process in place, rather we depend on our hosts to bring home information that may lead to intense cultivation."

Although the travel program does not directly increase major gifts, LeCouvie says there is an indirect benefit because of the engagement.

"A trip host is an excellent ambassador for the university and is able to speak about areas of need, interesting new research and current students," she says. "Our travelers generally are of an age that affords them luxuries, such as the trips, and more freedom to consider larger annual fund or major gifts."

Approximately 350 people participate in the travel program each year.

After the trip, the host shares any information that may indicate participants' proclivity to give with university fundraisers, who in turn determine whether to call on the prospect.

The Museum of Contemporary Art (MOCA) of Los Angeles, CA:

The travel program at MOCA is offered as a member benefit, with 40 to 50 people traveling to places like New York, Chicago, China, Germany and India each year.

"Our program is above all a donor benefit," says Veridiana Pontes-Ring, donor programs manager. "Our trips are exclusive and focus on giving participants the most exclusive VIP opportunities available and the best in contemporary art, design, hotel experience and cuisine."

Eligibility for local outings and day trips is for members contributing at the $650 level. Trips within the United States and to art fairs are for those contributing $1,500 and $4,500, while international trips are typically reserved for partners at the $10,000 level and trustees.

"MOCA travel is an important cultivation tool for the museum, providing an opportunity to spend time with our patrons and donors outside the museum and office in a unique art environment," Pontes-Ring says. "It has also proven to be an important benefit when members consider upgrading to MOCA Partner membership ($10,000)."

Additionally, she says, "the travel program gives members a sense of community and makes them feel like an active part of the museum. Members learn from higher-level donors and trustees, become friends and become active members of the MOCA community."

All members and visitors to the art museum benefit indirectly from the trips, says Pontes-Ring, as the ventures often lead to donations of artwork as well as donations to support exhibitions.

Sources: Leisha LeCouvie, Director of Parent and Affinity Programs, McGill University, Alumni Services, Montreal, Quebec, Canada. Phone (514) 398-1578. E-mail: leisha.lecouvie@mcgill.ca
Veridiana Pontes-Ring, The Museum of Contemporary Art, Los Angeles, CA. Phone (213) 621-1778. E-mail: mocatravel@moca.org

37. Second-ask Phonathon Raises More Than $18,000 for College

Development staff at Agnes Scott College (Decatur, GA) were in an enviable position with their alumnae challenge: They had secured enough donations to use all but $10,000 of matching funds available, up to $150,000. With some time left in the challenge, they decided to use the remaining funds as part of a phonathon to encourage prior donors to make a donation, offering the incentive of doubling the gift.

When the challenge money ran out one day before the phonathon, organizers chose to go ahead anyway and do a second ask to donors who had made gifts between July and December.

The result? They raised more than $18,000 in one night. They also secured 60 pledges and a record 34 credit card gifts in one night of calling.

Joanne Davis, director of the annual fund, says, "Callers were told to thank donors, tell them the college had a very ambitious annual fund goal and ask if they could help us reach it by making a second gift."

Through the experience, Davis says, she and her staff learned that while the reason for the alumnae challenge was to encourage lapsed donors and alumnae who had never given to do so, the majority of those participating in the challenge were those who had already made a gift.

Davis says they were disappointed to have missed reaching their target audience, but were pleased to find out alumnae who had already given were excited by the challenge and willing to give again.

Source: Joanne Davis, Director of the Annual Fund, Agnes Scott College, Decatur, GA. Phone (404) 471-5343. E-mail: jadavis@agnesscott.edu

38. Cookbook Auxiliary Wins Award, Boosts Sales

The Emerson Hospital Auxiliary (Concord, MA) has developed an award-winning cookbook that not only exceeded initial sales expectations, it is in its second printing.

The book "Revolutionary Recipes: Concord à la Carte" features 380 recipes that celebrate elegant, easy-to-prepare meals.

The cookbook committee, led by Beth Neeley-Kubacki, collected 1,500 recipes and selected, tested and tasted 500 of the best to determine which to showcase in the 398-page cookbook. Victor Lazzaro, a New England artist, created 10 original watercolor designs to complement the pages of the cookbook, while local writer Paula Williams developed a capsule history about each landmark featured throughout the pages.

To date, the auxiliary has printed 8,000 cookbooks and sold 6,000 at $24.95 each.

Published in 2002, the cookbook was the 2003 New England Regional Winner of the 14th annual Tabasco Community Cookbook Awards, solidifying its status as a fundraising success for the hospital. The award recognizes uniquely American cookbooks and committed volunteers who use it to benefit charitable causes.

The cookbook continues to be a popular income producer for the auxiliary, say auxiliary officials, who offer these tips to promote your organization's cookbook:

- Offer tastings of recipes at local venues and festivals.
- Host a meet-the-artists event where guests mingle with the artists and with writers who collaborated in the effort.
- Sell the cookbooks at tours of area homes and kitchens.
- Advertise cookbooks as holiday gift ideas and promote them at local inns, bookstores, museums, shops and historic homes.
- Try new venues for selling the cookbooks such as apple orchard stands and real estate offices. Think outside the box.

Source: Karen McCarthy, Vice President of Membership, Emerson Hospital Auxiliary, Concord, MA. Phone (978) 287-3019. E-mail: mccarthypp@aol.com

---

Key Ingredients to a Hot-selling Cookbook

Creating an award-winning cookbook involves key elements. Follow the example of Emerson Hospital Auxiliary (Concord, MA) by mixing in:

✓ **Phenomenal recipes.** The Emerson cookbook features Concord residents' easy-to-prepare recipes. Auxiliary members carefully tested, tasted and selected the best recipes out of 1,500 entries collected. Also, the recipes feature only fresh ingredients.

✓ **Visual impact.** The Revolutionary Recipes cookbook contains commissioned watercolor reproductions depicting historical regional landmarks.

✓ **Literary impact.** The cookbook also contains historical capsules of landmarks depicted throughout its pages.

✓ **Utility.** The design of the Revolutionary Recipes cookbook is hardcover with spiral binding within the cover creating a sturdy, useful and quality publication. The auxiliary intentionally designed a cookbook that has a washable cover, can lay flat for easy reading, offers large print for ease of reading and features one recipe per page.

---

39. **Advisory Boards Welcome Involvement, Lead to Major Gifts**

Identify and mine specific ways to connect individuals, businesses and industries to your organization to engage them in your cause.

Purdue University (West Lafayette, IN) hosts 34 industrial advisory boards that share research with corporate partners and build relationships that lead to funding.

Each advisory board is tied to a different field of research, such as food sciences, computer science, engineering education, and computer information and technology, says Betsy Liley, assistant vice president for corporate and foundation relations.

Liley says many of the boards are structured around membership levels, which range from $2,500 to $80,000 per year. Average group size is 15 to 20. These annual gifts help pay for the costs of running each board, including a salary for a paid staff member.

In addition to the annual membership gift, many companies sponsor research projects and fund scholarships for students in fields of interest to their advisory board, Liley says. While individual board structures vary, generally, each board sponsors research as a group, attends two meetings a year and may participate in annual job recruitment fairs.

"If the company's interest is in students and recruiting, they will be interested in supporting scholarships that will get them in front of students," she says. "If their interest is in research, they will want to sponsor research projects that expose them to our experts and allow them direct access to our research."

Advisory board members are at the corporate management level. Specific departments or colleges — many of which already have relationships with those departments or colleges through previous research funding — identify prospective corporate partners or attendance at job recruitment fairs on campus.

"Corporate involvement helps shape our curriculum, keeps us up to date on the skills our students need to have to compete in the job market, and guides our research," says Liley. "Our corporate partners have access to our research and our top students, and get to interact with their peers and partner with them on projects."

Source: Betsy Liley, Assistant Vice President for Corporate & Foundation Relations, Purdue University, West Lafayette, IN. Phone (765) 494-0635. E-mail: bliley@purdue.edu

Content not available in this edition

Advisory Board Attracts Corporate Funds

The Center for Education and Research in Information Assurance and Security (CERIAS) Industry Partnership Program is one of 34 corporate advisory boards at Purdue University (West Lafayette, IN).

CERIAS was formed in 1998, with the help of a Lily Foundation grant. Eugene H. Spafford, a professor of computer sciences at Purdue, is founder and executive director.

"CERIAS attracted Purdue faculty from 17 different departments and six different colleges," says Joel Rasmus, CERIAS director of strategic relations, who manages the Industry Partnership Program. "We're really here to help our faculty make connections to research companies and organizations, as well as being a single point of contact for the outside world to connect to the outstanding research that our faculty is doing."

The CERIAS Industry Partnership Program recognizes three tiers of donors (or members):

* $60,000 and up (all 11 members are at this level)
* $30,000 to $59,999
* $15,000 to $29,999 (geared to small Indiana start-ups)

"Companies are interested in partnering with us because they recognize the ever-growing threat of cyber security and want to keep up to date with advances taking place at Purdue," says Rasmus. "Many of these same companies fund direct research in this area (with 60-plus research projects currently under way). Their involvement with CERIAS gives them one place to call and connect with qualified faculty doing research in their interest areas. We also introduce them to our students, which gives them a leg up when it comes to hiring."

Tier one partners sit on the CERIAS External Advisory Board. CERIAS Industry Partnership members attend two meetings a year and are asked for assistance and guidance on emerging cyber security threats, new research areas, etc.

In addition to the annual membership fee, many companies provide funds for specific projects, he says.

"Our goal at the end of the year," Rasmus says, "is for each partner company to find it very easy to say that the relationship with CERIAS was absolutely worth the $60,000 investment, and that they want to continue the partnership."

Source: Joel Rasmus, Director of Strategic Relations, The CERIAS, Purdue University, West Lafayette, IN. Phone (765) 494-7806. E-mail: jrasmus@purdue.edu

40. Foundation Pins Fundraising Hopes on Jewelry Sales

It all started with one decorative jewelry pin, many years ago.

Created by Designs by Lucinda (Portland, ME), the pin was brought to the attention of the Wentworth-Douglass Hospital Foundation by its executive director who had sold the jewelry pieces to raise funds at her prior organization.

In the years since, sales of the pins have brought in nearly $20,000 for the foundation, says Mary Herring, foundation coordinator. The pins are sold at internal and external events, as well as displayed and sold at three different display cases throughout the hospital.

Here's how the program works: Organizations can contact Designs by Lucinda through the company's website (www.lucinda.com/fundraising) or by phone to order a minimum of 40 single-design pins, at $7.60 per pin. Officials with Designs by Lucinda recommend selling the pins for $16 each, for a 110 percent profit.

Placing an order by phone offers additional flexibility, letting you choose 60 pins in three styles with free shipping.

People who sport Lucinda pins become ambassadors for nonprofits through the conversations they start, according to the company's website.

Herring says she agrees with the pin's power to raise awareness, adding that the foundation is able to attach stickers to the card an which the pins are attached, allowing them to share more about their mission and activities.

Source: Mary Herring, Foundation Coordinator, Wentworth-Douglass Hospital Foundation, Dover, NH. Phone (603) 740-2581. E-mail: Mary.Herring@wdhospital.com

41. Text Donations Offer New Way to Talk About, Generate Gifts

In March 2010, staff at the Brooklyn Public Library (Brooklyn, NY) began accepting donations via text message. The undertaking was part of their Support Our Shelves campaign, an annual drive to raise money for library materials.

Jason Carey, director of marketing, says they thought text donations might attract potential donors for whom getting to the library is not always convenient. "We already had a separate texting technology to notify when materials were overdue, and when guests could pick up books," he says. "To introduce a donation element seemed like a natural progression."

- **How text donations work:** The Brooklyn Public Library chose to use mGive (a product of Mobile Accord, Denver, CO) — the same company that hosted text donations to victims of the Haitian earthquake. Donors use their phones to send a text to a predetermined number and specify how much they would like to donate. The system includes a widget for the library's website — donors click the widget and donate by entering a code. Additionally, mGive offers a Facebook widget, and other social networking tools to get the text donation program in public view.

- **Cost:** The library had to apply to be included in the service (see mGive's charitable participation standards, in the box, right) and pay a one-time setup fee of $500. Library staff then chose among three monthly packages ($399 bronze, $649 silver and $1,499 gold) and paid corresponding transaction fees (35 cents plus 3.5 percent bronze, 32 cents plus 3.5 percent silver or 30 cents plus 3.5 percent gold).

- **The Result:** Carey says the new program has produced modest results, but its implications are far-reaching. "The key thing we've seen so far is that it's a great way to get a new contingent of supporters involved with the library," he says. "It's a new way to talk about fundraising." By signing up for the program, potential donors are automatically put in contact with Carey and his marketing services; even the simple novelty of text-donation technology has attracted a new audience to cultivate as donors. Carey says he aims to add a sense of urgency to marketing for text donations. "When we give donors a reason to feel they need to give immediately, that will be the best way to utilize this as a tool."

Source: Jason Carey, Director of Marketing, Brooklyn Public Library, Brooklyn, NY. Phone (718)230-2209. E-mail: j.carey@brooklynpubliclibrary.org. Website: brooklynpubliclibrary.org

Content not available in this edition

42. Casting for a Cure Offers New Twists for Fishing Tourneys

The loss of loved ones to cancer brought a group of Minnesota residents together to create a new Minnesota-worthy event called Casting for a Cure (Sartell, MN).

Launched in September 2009, the event incorporates the joy of fishing and celebration of life for persons who experience cancer within their families. The event was founded by the children of Sandy Karasch, who died in 2008 from cancer. Joe Schulte, co-chair and Karasch's son-in-law, shares elements that contributed to the first-time event's success:

Specialty items. A commemorative fishing bobber with the event logo was made available on the event website, with 240 selling for $5 each.

PayPal donation options. Using the online money handling system, www.paypal.com, allowed website visitors to contribute. PayPal gifts ranged from $25 to $300.

Digital fishing competition. Participants paid a $30 fee, fished on any lake they wished, then photographed their catch using an official measuring tool and entered the photo.

Maximized exposure on social networking sites. Organizers spread the word about the event and donation options via Facebook and other social networking sites.

Special sponsor treatment. Sponsors donating $1,000 received a specialty gift basket.

Awards ceremony and silent auction. The awards celebration included a silent auction of fishing-related items which accounted for much of the event's funds.

Funds raised in the first-ever event allowed organizers to donate $15,000 to the Coborn Cancer Center (St. Cloud, MN) and create a perpetual fund for ongoing events. Plans for the 2010 event call for upgrading pro-fishing level giveaways for the tournament and fostering stronger relationships with sponsors.

Source: Joe Schulte, Co-Chair, Casting for a Cure-Greater Minnesota Fight for a Cure, Sartell, MN. Phone (320) 250-1010. E-mail: info@castingforacure.org. Website: www.castingforacure.org

---

Volunteer-created Spreadsheet Keeps Event Organized

Organizers of Casting for a Cure (Sartell, MN) focus on volunteers' strengths to generate the most efficient use of time and talents.

One such volunteer, Robyn Baker — an executive assistant by trade — formulated a spreadsheet using Microsoft Excel that identifies and tracks all incoming donations. Beyond the typical name and address information form, this spreadsheet (shown below) tracks follow-up calls, specific donation details, communications with donors and more.

"This spreadsheet format helped us quickly capture all the information we needed to efficiently capture sponsorship data and make sure there was no overlap across volunteers," says Tracy Schulte, event co-chair. "Having a single volunteer in charge of the spreadsheet made it reliable and accurate and easy to use as a starting place for the following year."

Source: Tracy Schulte, Co-Chair, Casting for a Cure-Greater Minnesota Fight for a Cure, Sartell, MN. Phone (320) 250-1010. E-mail: info@castingforacure.org

---

This sample shows the detailed format organizers of Casting for a Cure (Sartell, MN) use to track donor-related activity and better manage the special event.

Content not available in this edition

Content not available in this edition

43. Anniversary Lends Itself to Celebrating, Wooing Major Donors

When staff and supporters of the University of Southern California Thornton School of Music (Los Angeles, CA) began planning for its 125th anniversary two years ago, they began to think of every conceivable way to capitalize on the anniversary — and the number 125 — to attract gifts.

"Our message was that it may be our 125th anniversary, but that this was about building the next 125 years, and that takes resources," says Robert Cutietta, dean. "We decided early on to get everyone on board with our message about building our future. We weren't ashamed that our future included a need for money."

They planned concerts with 125 in the opus. They designed gifts with 125 in them, solicited a $1.25 million gift, eight $125,000 gifts, and encouraged alums to increase their $100 gifts to $125 in the spirit of the school's 125th anniversary. Over the course of the 125 days of celebration, the university hosted lectures, concerts or some type of event literally every day, says Cutietta.

"We planned a lot of high-profile events for people who give, which has provided many opportunities to showcase our donors," he says. "The campaign was very successful and a lot of fun. Everyone got into it."

Thirty-one days into the 125 days of celebration, the school held a celebratory dinner and concert that attracted 700 alumni and donors. "We wanted to hold our first large event fairly early into the celebration to show donors the kind of publicity the campaign would get," says Cutietta. Each gift was announced individually, followed by a two to three minute performance tied to the gift, e.g., if the gift was made to the piano program, a student played a short piano piece.

"Donors loved it," he says. "The event attracted more interest from prospective donors. Alums who hadn't been back for years made gifts of $1,250 instead of the $125 gifts we had asked for because they were inspired by the 125th anniversary."

Nearly halfway into the 125-day celebration, organizers raised $2.5 million, all from gifts that had the number 125 in them or were multiples of 125. Two of those gifts were matching gifts that were used to encourage additional $125 gifts, says Cutietta.

The celebration concluded with a formal gala dinner.

Donors who wished to be acknowledged at the Dec. 11 event had to make their gift by that date.

The cultivation and solicitation of major donors was done almost exclusively in person. No written proposals were used. "My wife and I invited one or two couples to dinner, and small groups of donors were invited to a special dinner before certain events," he says.

> "We planned a lot of high-profile events for people who gave, which provided many opportunities to showcase our donors."

Alums received three mailings over nine months. The first alerted them of the 125th anniversary celebrations. The second announced the launch of the celebration and invited them to return to campus for anniversary-related events. Neither of the first two mailings included a solicitation. The third mailing included a specific ask.

No printed material was produced specifically for the campaign. Instead, 125th anniversary logos were added to existing materials. School officials created gifts instead, including crystal glasses and computer jump drives with the 125th anniversary logo.

The 125 days of celebration has provided numerous opportunities for media coverage, including a full-page spread in the LA Times, as well as articles in targeted music publications. "We did very focused announcements about different programs at the school that would be attractive to specific publications," Cutietta says. "For example, we talked about jazz gifts to the jazz world and piano gifts to the piano world."

The keys to their success were starting really early with the planning and deciding early on what their message would be, says Cutietta: "Our focused, simple message really captivated people. We also got everyone on board internally first and hired an outside firm to help keep us focused. It helped to have an outsider who didn't know anything about the internal politics and limitations involved."

Source: Robert Cutietta, Dean, USC Thornton School of Music, Los Angeles, CA. Phone (213) 740-5389.
E-mail: MusicDean@Thornton.usc.edu

44. Progressive Strolls Raise Awareness, Annual Funds

Officials with the Stuhr Museum Foundation, which supports the Stuhr Museum of the Prairie Pioneer (Grand Island, NE), held four progressive strolls in its 1890s Living History Railroad Town in 2009.

The strolls raised awareness for museum programs and gifts for its annual fund.

Some 196 people attended the strolls, including 113 new and renewed donors, far surpassing the organizers' goal of increasing new and renewed annual fund donors, says Pam Price, executive director. Museum and foundation trustee host couples underwrote stroll costs.

Participants strolled through the museum's recreated railroad town and enjoyed authentic "savories" (1890s-speak for hors d'oeuvres) beer, wine and bottled water.

Price says each evening stroll required at least 20 staff, including a costumed interpreter to greet guests at each location to tell them about the structure. Two additional staff persons spoke on their positions with the museum, while trustees or host couples served as group leaders.

The campaign's co-chairs made the ask at the stroll's last stop.

"We spoke of the theme, campaign goal and our focus on recruiting new donors to the campaign," she says. "The campaign chairs were impressive, speaking from their hearts with their asks. Also, museum staff members were very effective in their roles, speaking from their depth of knowledge and passion for their programs."

Organizers told attendees that the foundation would mail campaign materials in two or three days. They also had pledge cards and membership materials on hand.

For the first stroll, couples currently involved in the museum and foundation invited friends who were not members or donors. The second and third strolls invited current donors to attend with the cost of their admission being to bring a friend who was a non-donor. The last stroll targeted the chamber of commerce's young professionals group and young entrepreneurs recently honored by the chamber. Invitations to this last group were sent via e-mail rather than the traditional invitation used for the first three events.

Source: Pamela L. Price, Executive Director, Stuhr Living History Museum Foundation, Grand Island, NE. Phone (308) 385-5131. E-mail: pprice@stuhrmuseum.org

 ## 45. Involve Younger Constituents at a Summer Beach Party

Summer is vacation time for many potential donors, making it the perfect time for your organization to host a summer-fun fundraiser that celebrates your organization while attracting new donors.

Brian Kish, assistant vice president for advancement at Salve Regina University (Newport, RI) and annual giving consultant with Campbell & Company (Chicago, IL), says that one of the most important ways to promote annual giving is to attract younger donors.

"The earlier you can start engaging potential donors, the better," Kish says. The likelihood of a donor returning to donate to the same institution increases approximately 20 percent with each year of his/her engagement.

One proven way to attract younger people — both current and future donors — is to plan a fundraiser around an event they would want to attend anyway, Kish says. "You want people to be asking one another, 'Are you going to this event? Well, then so am I.'"

Salve Regina hosts The Bash at the Beach — a seaside party in a historical and touristy part of town, he says. "We knew younger alumni would be around town during the summer, but wouldn't be coming to campus. So we decided to take the fundraising party to them."

For a summer bash, Kish recommends:

✓ Holding the event at a well-loved restaurant or bar with outdoor seating, a large deck or a waterfront view.

✓ Charging a ticket price that serves as the donor's contribution to the fundraiser. The ticket will earn the donor two drinks, food, parking, and a gift. Build the fair market value of those items into the ticket price, with enough left over to earn a healthy percentage for your organization.

✓ Aiming your marketing techniques at younger donors — advertise in recent alumni publications, organizations for young professionals and online.

Source: Brian Kish, Assistant Vice President for Advancement, Salve Regina University, Newport, RI, and Annual Giving Consultant, Campbell & Company, Chicago, IL. Phone (401) 847-6650. E-mail: annualGiving@campbellcompany.com and brian.kish@salve.edu. Websites: www.salve.edu and www.campbellcompany.com/people/b_kish.html

46. Pooling Major Donors' Gifts Adds Up for Giving Group, Hospital Foundation

St. Joseph's Hospital Foundation (Tampa, FL) is reaching out to philanthropic women through a new group called Philanthropic Women of St. Joseph's. The leadership network of community-minded women has a mission of changing and saving lives in the Tampa Bay community by investing in collaboration with other women leaders.

Members' annual philanthropic contributions are pooled and they decide together which St. Joseph's Hospital project to fund each year.

The group's two founders hand-selected a steering committee, whose members were asked to recruit their friends. "It spread like wildfire," says Gunn. "Women were attracted by the ability to pool their gifts to increase the impact of their $1,000 gift. They also liked the idea of sharing experiences and health education with like-minded, entrepreneurial women."

The group offers three membership levels:

- **Founder:** A $25,000 commitment paid over one to five years. Founder members receive permanent recognition as Philanthropic Women of St. Joseph's and are permanent members of the steering committee.
- **Leader:** A $10,000 commitment paid over one to five years. Members receive recognition as Philanthropic Women Leaders for the length of their pledge and may serve a two-year term as a steering committee member.
- **Member:** A $1,000 annual commitment.

Membership currently includes two at the founder level, nine at the leader level and 55 at the member level, Gunn says.

Each year, the membership is presented with three possible projects to fund. The three projects are based on the hospital's funding priorities. The steering committee researches each project, presents them to the entire group, and the group votes on which project to fund.

Members are encouraged to attend three scheduled meetings per year: a speaker's luncheon, which serves as the group's membership drive; a project selection meeting in which the group votes on which project to fund; and a celebration that includes a presentation by those who were impacted by the gift. The latter two meetings are held in a member's home.

"The group has appreciated the fact that they can be as involved as they would like," says Gunn. "For those looking to build a strong allegiance to their nonprofit, this is absolutely the right structure. We have made many friends we otherwise wouldn't have known had an interest in our organization. It's also a great way to build a donor base for future major gifts."

Source: Nora Gunn, Director of Development, St. Joseph's Hospital Foundation, Tampa, FL. Phone (813) 872-0979.
E-mail: nora.gunn@baycare.org

Founding the Philanthropic Women of St. Joseph's

With generous gifts of $25,000 each, Donna Jordan and Elaine F. Shimberg founded Philanthropic Women of St. Joseph's (PWSJ), a giving group that supports St. Joseph's Hospital Foundation (Tampa, FL).

The founders receive permanent recognition as Philanthropic Women and are permanent members of the group's steering committee. Their gifts are pooled with other members' and together the entire membership chooses a funding project to support each year.

"After becoming a foundation board member, I was presented with the most exciting challenge of all: Philanthropic Women of St. Joseph's Hospital," says Jordan.

"This endeavor had not been done with any hospital in our area; we would be the first. Also, it was an opportunity to work with my mentor, Elaine Shimberg," she says. "Through the PWSJ, my commitment has become stronger than ever. It has given me an opportunity to bring in friends, old and new, and to introduce them to and educate them about the mission of St. Joseph's Hospital. We have had opportunities to meet doctors, nurses and administrative staff and learn the latest in cutting-edge technology as well as specific needs of the hospital."

Jordan says the philanthropic group also allows them "to bring in talented women in our area who otherwise might not have been involved in the hospital unless they were faced with a specific health need. These women we bring in will, in turn, bring their friends and acquaintances into the St. Joseph's family. It's been an exciting and fulfilling time."

Shimberg has served as a volunteer at St. Joseph's Hospitals for more than 25 years, serving on several hospital committees and as chair of the hospital's board of trustees. She currently serves as chair of the St. Joseph's Hospital Foundation Board.

"I loved the idea of Philanthropic Women of St. Joseph's because it was a way to bring in new faces and helping hands," Shimberg says. "I knew that the more our community's young women knew about St. Joseph's Hospital, the more they'd want to continue their involvement and enjoy supporting it financially. Having Donna Jordan as a co-founder has infused the group with an amazing energy and enthusiasm.

"It has strengthened my commitment to the hospital because it reminds me of why I got involved so many years ago . Lastly, I must admit, the energy of our PWSJ members has recharged my batteries as well. It's fun!"

Sources: Donna Jordan, Founder, and Elaine F. Shimberg, Founder, Philanthropic Women of St. Joseph's, St. Joseph's Hospital Foundation, Tampa, FL. Phone (813) 872-0979.
E-mail: sjhfoundation@baycare.org

47. Selling Christmas Trees? Double Your Revenue

Selling Christmas trees may seem like a holiday fundraising no-brainer. After all, trees are traditionally regarded as high-profit items, whether sold commercially or to benefit a nonprofit organization.

But with a little creative brain power, you can watch your tree sales proceeds really grow.

That's what Bob McIntyre learned when he organized the annual Christmas tree sale at the Dor-Wood Optimist Club (Kettering, OH), a nonprofit dedicated to youth development.

McIntyre says that his first year in charge of the tree sale, he doubled the previous year's profits, from $9,500 to more than $19,000 — and earned that amount in only a three-and-a-half week period. Not only that, he says, but the Optimist International lot managed to post such profits even with competition of a commercial tree lot 200 yards down the street. "We drove them nuts," McIntyre says of the commercial operation, "because we were able to beat anything available from commercial providers."

McIntyre, who has a professional background in sales, says to grow profits, he focused on "expenses and opportunities for new markets."

Here are the changes McIntyre made to the sales strategy that led to such a drastic profit increase:

❑ Taking pre-orders for large, custom trees and wreaths for hospitals and corporations.

❑ Delivering and setting up trees and wreaths if requested.

❑ Changing suppliers to a less-expensive grower. (McIntyre admits, "I crossed my fingers that the quality would be good. It was.")

❑ Running an ad in the local weekly paper with a coupon for $5 off a tree.

❑ Impressing upon the volunteer sales staff that, "As of Dec. 26, it was mulch, and they should make sure that we sold everything."

When McIntyre organized the Christmas tree sales for the second year, the event posted more than $20,000 in profits.

Source: Bob McIntyre, Kettering Dor-Wood Optimist Club, Kettering, OH. Phone (937) 237-9428.
E-mail: jailandbail@dorwood.com. Website: www.dorwood.com

48. Holiday Gift Wrap Raises Funds, Involves Community

The weeks between Thanksgiving and Christmas mean many things to many people, but to the residents of Cheyenne, WY, they mean volunteers from the Cheyenne Regional Medical Center will be wrapping piles of holiday gifts both day and night at the local mall.

"We're in our 29th year and still going strong," says Bev Catalano, volunteer director at the center. "It's a service that's well-known in the community and very popular."

Well-stocked with festive paper, bows and ribbon, volunteers wrap some 3,000 to 5,000 gifts in any given year, most for a fee of $3 to $5. And though center officials pay a minimum deposit and percentage of sales to the mall for use of an empty storefront or central booth, they still clear $10,000 to $17,000 every year.

What is the most difficult part of hosting a month-long fundraiser?

"Volunteers," says Catalano without hesitation. Though 100 or so are drawn from the center's active volunteer base, 150 more must be recruited from the community itself.

To meet this need, each of the fundraiser's almost 30 days has a day chair responsible for ensuring the booth is adequately staffed with workers.

Many of these volunteers come from the hospital staff itself, but day chairs also network through churches, clubs and other employers.

Because the three-decade-old event is well-known in the area, Catalano notes, it often draws groups of volunteers such as the employees of a bank, the members of a sorority or the staff of a local newspaper.

Though the fundraiser demands significant human resources, Catalano cites not only the sheer fun of holiday festivities, but also the chance to interact with the wider community as some of the benefits making the effort worthwhile.

"People's first question is always the cause we are raising money for," she says. "The gift wrap provides a great opportunity to increase awareness about the projects we're working on and the services we provide to the community."

Source: Bev Catalano, Volunteer Director, Cheyenne Regional Medical Center, Cheyenne, WY. Phone (307) 633-7513.
E-mail: Bev.catalano@crmcwy.org

49. **Relationships Bloom With Executive Offerings**

Consider creating a giving venue for a select group of your current or future supporters.

At Make-A-Wish Foundation of Illinois (Chicago, IL), Susan Schultze, manager of annual and leadership giving, and her colleagues were looking for a way to boost their individual giving when they developed their Executives for Make-A-Wish Network.

"Our individual giving was one of the areas we wanted to increase, and we were looking for a way to find people who have the heart for Make-A-Wish and the capacity to support our mission," Schultze explains.

So they decided to reach out to executives from companies that were already supporting the foundation, asking them each to make a $15,000 commitment over a three-year period to grant the wishes of three local children. Foundation representatives asked for the gifts to be personal gifts from the individual executives, hoping to use the network as a platform to transition members to longer-term individual giving.

"The idea to offer business forums and networking opportunities was taken straight from our local economic club," says Schultze. "They have these amazing business forums that are highly attended because of the speakers and the topics. We thought we could offer something similar, giving those who committed to the network access to other leaders in the community, along with high visibility for them as professionals supporting our organization."

Members of Make-A-Wish's executive network receive invitations to two gatherings per year that foster networking and give members access to other successful executives. They also receive invitations to the foundation's VIP and exclusive donor receptions, along with exposure for them as professionals in program booklets for the Wish Ball Gala, golf outing and donor luncheon events.

One third of the executives invited attended the network's initial meeting, with 11 committing to the network within the first year, raising $165,000 for the foundation, Schultze says. In addition, one of the executives generated another $50,000 in leads.

Funds raised made it possible for 33 children with life-threatening medical conditions to have their wishes granted through the foundation.

Source: Susan Schultze, Annual and Leadership Giving, Make-A-Wish Foundation of Illinois, Chicago, IL. Phone (312) 602-9427. E-mail: schultze@wishes.org

Ongoing Evaluation Important in Executive Network

While the initial offering of the Executives for Make-A-Wish Network was successful, Susan Schultze, manager of annual and leadership giving, Make-A-Wish Foundation of Illinois (Chicago, IL), says the program's ongoing success depends on continual evaluation of which executives are good prospects for individual versus corporate giving and whether the two types of giving can be separated.

Schultze and her colleagues have determined that many executives initially involved through the corporate program detailed above ultimately continue to support the organization and have a significant tie to the mission.

However, she says, the internal analysis also shows these executives tend to make their gifts through their company, allowing them to highlight their company involvement and support the organization at the same time. Plus, some executives had been making gifts at higher levels through their workplace giving programs prior to joining the network.

Schultze says this kind of evaluation ensures that the Make-A-Wish outreach and cultivation is accomplishing its goals. It also offers the opportunity to determine if there is a better way to engage those individuals.

"The Executives for Make-A-Wish Network did engage a few new people and offered existing supporters an additional way to engage," she notes. "Since the inception of the network, we have worked with these executives one-on-one to create partnerships that make sense on both sides of the table."

50. Donors Support Professionals With Endowed Lecture Series

The University of Texas M.D. Anderson Cancer Center (Houston, TX) currently has 20 endowed lecture series.

"An endowed lecture series is a great way for a donor to give money to help a department complement its professional development for faculty and students," says Fernando A. Yarrito, senior director of constituent relations and stewardship.

Donors of endowed lecture series are invited to attend the lectures and luncheons that may follow.

"Participation in the lecture is a good way to keep the donor involved," Yarrito says. Those who cannot attend receive a copy of the flyer distributed at the lectures.

While the minimum amount needed to fund an endowed lecture series is currently $50,000, in the past it was as little as $20,000, says Yarrito, so their current endowed lecture series amounts range from $20,000 to $100,000.

"The more donor funds we have, the higher amount of interest income generated and available for funding the series," he says. "We encourage donors to give at a higher level so that there is more to spend each year to produce a series. A $20,000 endowed lecture series may not generate enough to produce a series each year."

Lecture series endowments are established as a result of a direct desire of a donor to support a particular faculty member, department or program, says Yarrito.

"While we truly appreciate these endowments, recently we have turned our focus to increasing academic positions (chairs, professorships)," he says.

"M.D. Anderson Cancer Center is a large hospital with thousands of employees," says Yarrito. "It is difficult for the development office to manage a lecture series in another department. As a stewardship objective, however, we make every effort to offer guidance and support to these departments in order for these lectures to be as informative and effective as the donor intended."

Source: Fernando A. Yarrito, Senior Director of Constituent Relations & Stewardship, University of Texas M.D. Anderson Cancer Center, Houston, TX. Phone (713) 563-4061. E-mail: fayarrito@mdanderson.org

51. Four Keys to Raising Money in Lean Times

In fiscal 2008-2009, as charitable contributions to universities fell by 12 percent, the University of Missouri-St. Louis (St. Louis, MO) posted a 54 percent increase in annual giving.

Martin Leifeld, vice chancellor of university advancement, attributes that success in large part to refusing to be fearful when fundraising in hard times. He shares four areas fundraisers should focus on to succeed in tough economic conditions:

1. **Deferred pledges, structured payments.** Shrinking portfolios change the amount of resources at donors' disposal, but not the basic level at which they wish to give, says Leifeld. The key is offering planned giving solutions that allow them to reach the level to which they are accustomed by being creative, such as crafting a multi-year payment option rather than an outright gift.

2. **Patience and expanded time horizons.** Leifeld says fundraising simply takes longer in a bad economy. "Because the process is more complicated for donors, major gift fundraisers just have to be patient. That doesn't mean you are passive, but you do have to shift your thinking to be respectful of the position donors are in."

3. **A relentless focus on major gifts.** Facing a tough fundraising environment, Leifeld and staff maintained a disciplined focus on $250,000-plus gifts. They created a display in his office of every major gift under way with associated financial numbers, anticipated close date and assigned gift officer; met monthly with gift officers to discuss every major gift; and roll-played rehearsals prior to major donor meetings.

4. **An opportunistic mentality.** "Every day you need to be looking for the opportunities of the moment," he says. "Lately, donors seem more interested in helping people with scholarship and programming endowments than in putting names on buildings. You still have your capital priorities, of course, but you can't afford to ignore enthusiasm anywhere you find it. At the end of the day, fundraisers have to be social observers, noting and understanding what is going on in the wider frame of society."

Source: Martin Leifeld, Vice Chancellor of University Advancement, University of Missouri-St. Louis, St. Louis, MO. Phone (314) 516-4151. E-mail: Leifeldm@umsl.edu

52. ## Giving Club Revamp Puts Emphasis on Long-term Intent

Andrea Meloan, director of the Jewell Fund, William Jewell College (Liberty, MO), says its previous leadership giving society was not as effective as they would have liked.

"Donors seemed too focused on the first-time member benefit (a brick inscribed with their name installed in the Quadrangle, our main part of campus), and we had more lapsed leadership-level donors than we were comfortable with," Meloan says.

Development staff recognized the need for a new society that better emphasized the importance of leadership gifts to the college's annual fund over the long term — and the John Priest Greene Society was born.

This new society honors the legacy of Jewell's longest-serving president, hoping to get donors to make a long-term commitment to the college as well. Meloan says the goal is to increase the number of donors who give at the leadership level on an annual basis. "New members join the society after they make a multi-year commitment or a sustaining (until further notice) commitment to the Jewell Fund."

John Priest Greene Society members are expected to make an annual leadership gift of at least $1,000 to the Jewell Fund, at any point during the college's fiscal year. They also refer prospective students, promote the mission of the college in their communities and encourage others to support Jewell in similar ways.

For their contributions, members receive a members-only quarterly newsletter from the president, invitation to an annual president's reception and recognition in the annual Honor Roll of Donors report. First-time leadership level donors still receive the inscribed brick on the Quad, which becomes a permanent part of Jewell — something Meloan says she hopes the donor will become, too. "We worked to come up with a name for the society that would reflect what this group of people represents for the college — service and support that will have a lasting effect on strengthening Jewell for future generations."

Source: Andrea Meloan, Director of the Jewell Fund, William Jewell College, Liberty, MO. Phone (816) 415-7831.
E-mail: meloana@william.jewell.edu

Five Ways to Promote New Gift Societies

Marketing was critical to getting the word out when they created their new leadership giving society Andrea Meloan, director of the Jewell Fund, William Jewell College (Liberty, MO), says. "We not only had to market to alumni and potential members," Meloan says, "we also had to educate past giving society members on what the new society is and how it differs from our former program."

Meloan's staff continues using the following strategies to ensure their constituents know about the new John Priest Greene Society:

1. Completing personal follow-up with recipients of the invitation to join the society, including meetings, e-mails and phone calls. The student call center also contacts those who don't respond by a given date.

2. Holding one-on-one meetings to provide information about the college today, share its hopes for the future and ask for a wide variety of feedback, including individuals' charitable priorities and knowledge of giving programs like the new society.

3. Creating and distributing a quarterly newsletter from the college's president that provides small chunks of campus news that is unique to any other communication they distribute and is easy to read.

4. Visiting members in person when possible.

5. Promoting the society with feature stories and full-page promotional pieces in the college's various publications.

Meloan says it's important not to stop at mass-marketing measures. "Reach out and follow-up to talk about the new giving society in one-on-one and small group settings as often as possible. This cements the importance of the giving society and encourages feedback about your organization and the future likelihood of individuals to join the new society."

53. Program Club Boosts Good Will and Giving

What started as a simple marketing idea has turned into a way to increase revenue and build better relationships with supporters, says Elise Marquam-Jahns, director of planned giving, Twin Cities Public Television, Inc. (St. Paul, MN).

The *tpt*-PBS Program Club is like a book club, with members discussing public television programming rather than the latest bestseller. Members choose from six program clubs — one that meets monthly at the station June through November, and five that meet at Twin Cities-area senior complexes October through June.

People watch a selected show at home and visit a club meeting to discuss it with other participants. Those who attend the station club also hear behind-the-scenes information from a staff person, including producers talking about their latest local or national productions.

Marquam-Jahns says members "enjoy the learning opportunities, the chance to meet others who have similar interests and the chance to make new friends."

The club has also helped the TV station increase revenue. Says Marquam-Jahns, "Many individuals who were $25 to $50 annual supporters have become major donors and/or planned giving donors. Since the club began, 31 Program Club members have become Visionary Society members, including *tpt* in their will or estate plan."

Over the past three years, she says, the giving club has increased fundraising revenue in the following ways:

✓ 86 percent of regular attendees have increased their annual giving.

✓ 68 percent have increased their annual giving by 50 percent or more.

✓ 36 percent have joined the Studio Society, *tpt*'s major donor organization.

✓ 23 percent included *tpt* in their wills.

✓ 9 percent have made charitable gift annuities.

Interested in starting a similar program? "Give it some time to develop," says Marquam-Jahns. "We started with a core group of eight people. Now we have 50 to 60 who attend the club at the station each month and over 125 attending at the senior centers."

Source: Elise Marquam-Jahns, Director of Planned Giving, Twin Cities Public Television, Inc., St. Paul, MN. Phone (651) 229-1276. E-mail: emjahns@tpt.org. Website: www.tpt.org

 ### 54. Committee Empowers Donors

Donors are unique in the ways they give and in what motivates them to give.

One Iowa foundation has found a way to celebrate the distinct giving trends of one group of donors while reaping the benefits.

For nine years, the Iowa State University (ISU) Foundation (Ames, IA) has invited female donors to serve on its women and philanthropy committee and act as advocates for ISU and for philanthropy.

Women chosen to serve are interested in philanthropy and interested in empowering women, says Melissa Hanna, executive director of annual and special giving.

The committee hosts an annual women and philanthropy workshop where, through keynote speakers and breakout sessions, women learn about creating and maintaining healthy financial positions.

"The committee definitely brings women to the forefront," Hanna says. "We want to focus more attention on that constituency and make sure their philanthropic needs are met. We want women to feel empowered and know they have a voice in this discussion as well."

The proof of the committee's efforts is in the numbers. According to Hanna:

✓ The foundation experienced a 47 percent increase in total number of women donors since 2000. The number jumped from 72,095 women donors by Dec. 31, 2000, to 105,816 by Dec. 31, 2008.

✓ Since 2003, Iowa State saw a 240 percent increase in total dollars given by women, increasing from $10,844,807 in fiscal year 2003 to $36,824,280 in fiscal year 2008.

✓ The average gift from a woman also increased 184 percent from $597 in FY 2003 to $1,696 in FY 2008.

✓ Through 2008, women have given more than $218 million to ISU.

The women and philanthropy committee comprises 17 women from varying professions, all with an interest in ISU. Members may serve two, two-year terms, with those holding the position of board chair granted an extra term. The committee typically meets five times a school year with the first meeting being a fall retreat.

Source: Melissa Hanna, Executive Director of Annual and Special Giving, Iowa State University Foundation, Ames, Iowa. Phone (515) 294-0596. E-mail: mhanna@foundation.iastate.edu

55. Passport Helps Transport Wine Tasting Into Profitable Event

An annual wine tasting for the Cal State Fullerton Alumni Association (Fullerton, CA) may have been an exclusive, high-end, big-ticket event beloved by board members and volunteers alike, but it was losing $14,000 a year.

Something had to change, says Dianna Fisher, executive director.

"Facing a state budget collapse, we knew we had to look at the cost effectiveness, outreach potential and strategic purpose of every activity," she says. "Lowering the price point, expanding attendance and strengthening the philanthropic component were crucial."

Organizers added a silent auction, lowered the ticket price to $55 per person, and traded a sit-down dinner for appetizer food stations. The result was a 2010 event that not only doubled the previous year's attendance, but for the first time broke even on operating expenses and raised $9,000 in scholarship revenue.

Central to the event's success was the decidedly international flair of the eight food stations that Fisher says made the event as much a food tasting as a wine tasting. Also key was inviting a certified sommelier to pair wines to meals and explain the pairings to guests, says Fisher. She notes the Zinfandel/Shiraz and home-style barbeque was a particularly popular pairing.

They also kept costs low in a conscious effort to attract new alumni, Fisher says. "We showcased some unusual wines, but the majority were comparable to what someone might buy at the corner shop and actually serve with dinner.

They also kept auction items' values at a lower level than previous events to allow more attendees to experience the excitement of bidding.

The fundraiser sold out its 180-person venue and grossed more than $18,000.

Source: Dianna Fisher, Executive Director, California State University, Fullerton Alumni Association, Fullerton, CA. Phone (657) 278-2586. E-mail: Difisher@fullerton.edu

Content not available in this edition

Create Interactive Donor Wall

RCB Awards (Milwaukee, WI) has developed an interactive donor recognition option that combines a traditional static donor wall with a functional and engaging electronic multimedia presentation.

The wall's interactive video touch screens allow an organization to create a personalized project by incorporating videos depicting its mission and programs, as well as donor stories and other elements.

"A good donor wall should be more than a list of names; it should be a showcase of your most significant achievements, an acknowledgement of your most generous supporters and a powerful statement about your purpose and vision," says Curt Denevan, sales and marketing manager. "It should be the first step in soliciting campaign donors. The viewer of every donor wall is a prospective donor of your organization. Does your wall talk to them?"

Design options allow organizations to create a wall with one large touch screen and/or several smaller touch screens. Cost depends on size, type of material used, number and size of touch screens and other elements. View a sample interactive donor wall at: www.youtube.com/watch?v=MgUK1qgwa7c

Source: Curt Denevan, Sales & Marketing Manager, RCB Awards, Milwaukee, WI. Phone (414) 479-9100. E-mail: curtd@rcbawards.com. Website: www.rcbdonorrecognition.com

57. Breakfast Galas Boost Fundraising, Recruitment Efforts

Prospective donors and volunteers have a deluge of gala dinners, walkathons, auctions and similar events to choose from when deciding where to give their time, money and attention.

To stand out from that pack, consider organizing a breakfast gala.

When staff of the Capital Breast Care Center (CBCC), a community health center in Washington, DC, began brainstorming its first-ever large fundraising event, "We opted not to go with an evening event, because in my opinion there are just so many of them," says Beth Beck, executive director. "Very few do breakfast events, so we could be unique in that way."

The CBCC's annual breakfast gala raised $50,000 the first year and $100,000 in both its second and third years.

In addition to being a unique event to put on one's social calendar, there are two additional ways that a breakfast gala may be a better choice than other types of fundraising events, Beck says:

❏ **Guaranteed time commitment for guests.** As opposed to dinner receptions — which have the reputation of going on too long because of entertainment or an over-extended cocktail hour — a breakfast gala, by its very nature, will be run on a tight schedule. It promotes a warm yet get-down-to-business ambiance, Beck says. The CBCC's breakfast gala lasts exactly one hour. Because it sticks to its schedule, attendees are pleased with the event and are more likely to return the following year, bringing along more of their friends, family and community members as prospective donors. Beck says attendance at the CBCC's breakfast has increased each year by about 100 people.

❏ **Guaranteed time period for planning purposes.** Because the event does not run over schedule, the event

---

Punch Up Pledge Card Power

Look for multiple ways to share your message and your need with your event attendees.

At the annual breakfast gala for the Capital Breast Care Center (CBCC), Washington, DC, for example, in addition to watching a moving video to encourage increased donations, attendees receive pledge cards that detail different ask amounts, and what each amount will provide at the center. For example, next to the box a donor would check if he/she was pledging $50 is the statement: "$50 will provide one woman with her annual mammogram."

Helping donors visualize how their money will be allocated — and how it will directly impact another person's life for the better — is a powerful way to increase donations and, ultimately, awareness of the good your cause does.

---

leaders hold the attention of the attendees throughout the program. Therefore, when the CBCC plans its breakfast, it can build up attention over the course of the hour, rather than worry about losing people's attention. "Right before our ask at the end of the event, we show a video in which a woman speaks about the care she received at the center. It creates a personal connection and allows people to really understand what the center does. Even though the video comes at the end of the event, it is the most powerful moment."

Beth Beck, Executive Director, Capital Breast Care Center, Washington, DC. Phone (202) 870-1139. E-mail: info@capitalbreastcare.org. Website: www.capitalbreastcare.org

58. Gift Memberships Engage Current Members, Attract Newcomers

Offering gift memberships can be an effective way to grow your member-based organization. Here are examples of how two organizations are finding success doing so:

American Homebrewers Association (Boulder, CO):

Persons who want to give a one-year gift membership ($38) to the American Homebrewers Association (AHA) purchase an AHA gift card on the association's website.
The gift cards have increased gift memberships by 300 percent, says Director Gary Glass.

The gift card is affixed to a mailable paper holder that contains To and From fields and an area for personalization. The gift card/holder is mailed to the gift giver, who then mails it to the gift membership recipient. The recipient visits a website and uses a code printed on the gift card to validate the membership. Once a gift membership is validated, the person receiving it is mailed a new member packet.

Glass says they originally used the gift cards in home brew supply stores to attract new members, but their ease of use prompted AHA officials to start using the cards for gift memberships about two years ago.

"Rather than having the member give us the gift member's contact information and mailing address, the person who receives the gift card fills out their information, which reduces the chance of errors," Glass says. "It also allows us to shorten the turnaround time to process a gift membership from three weeks to three days. All we have to do is mail out a gift card/card holder to the gift giver and they do the rest."

AHA's gift cards are produced by Advanced Labeling Systems (Denver, CO) and cost about $1,200 for 2,500, plus mailing cost of 44 cents each. View a sample at: www.homebrewersassociation.org/attachments/0000/1500/GIFT-CARD.jpg

Adventure Cycling Association (Missoula, MT):

The annual Share the Cycling Joy membership recruitment campaign for the Adventure Cycling Association (Missoula, MT) has increased gift memberships by 25 percent in two years, says Julie Huck, membership director. The year-round effort offers members the opportunity to win prizes — including a shopping spree at the association's online gift shop — for giving gift memberships and/or encouraging cyclists to join.

"We pulled together existing elements like our send-a-friend sample issue and holiday gift programs and developed the Share the Cycling Joy program around them," Huck says. "Because of the time it takes to develop the infrastructure for this type of system, an important part of creating it was the ability to use it for multiple years."

Members participate by giving a gift membership ($40 except October-December, when cost is $20; see story, below) or by using an online form to send a sample issue of the association's magazine or e-mail that allows a friend to request a free issue.

"Sending the sample issue encourages the most cyclists to join," Huck notes.

The association promotes the gift membership campaign with a member magazine ad, article in its bi-weekly e-newsletter to 40,000 member and non-member subscribers, on its website (www.adventurecycling.org/joy), in blog posts, on the association's Facebook page, in an October e-mail and a printed piece in November.

The retention rate for members who join through the campaign is about 28 percent.

Sources: Julie Huck, Membership & Development Director, Adventure Cycling Association, Missoula, MT.
Phone (800) 755-2453 ext. 214. E-mail: jhuck@adventurecycling.org
Gary Glass, Director, American Homebrewer's Association, Boulder, CO. Phone (888) 822-6273, ext. 121.
E-mail: gary@brewerassociation.org

Limited-time Appeal Encourages Gift Memberships

Persons who wish to give a gift membership to the Adventure Cycling Association (Missoula, MT) can do so year-round for $40 (see story, above). But each October through December, they can make the same gift at half the price — just in time for holiday gift giving, says Julie Huck, membership director.

"We promote our holiday gift membership program through e-mail, with messages in our e-newsletter and with a mailing piece sent to members in November," Huck says. The mailing piece includes a letter introducing the program, a form to renew their membership and give gifts and a return envelope.

Gift membership recipients receive a card with a personal message from the donor and membership card prior to receiving their new member packet, which is mailed about a week later.

In January, new gift members who joined during the holiday campaign receive a special welcome e-mail.

In 2009, new and renewing members gave 462 gift memberships (275 at half price and 187 at full price) during the association's holiday gift membership program, says Huck, noting that the retention rate among gift members is about 28 percent.

59. **Tune In a TV-themed Event**

What do you get when you mix the Dixieland stars-and-bars of "Dukes of Hazzard," elegant candelabras of "Dynasty," and khaki fatigues of "M*A*S*H"?

If you're the Rotary Club of Pottsville (Pottsville, PA), you get TV Night in Pottsville, the theme of its second annual Necho Allen Night fundraiser dinner. The 2010 event drew 200 participants and raised $2,800 for four local charities.

Mary Sitcoske, club secretary, says guests pay $25 for a night of TV-themed fun featuring complimentary beverages, music from a professional DJ and a small Chinese auction.

But the evening's top features are the costumes and table decorations. TV dramas, sitcoms, commercials and sports teams all have their supporters, and competition is stiff for awards such as best costume, most original idea and most creative presentation of theme.

For people uncomfortable with the idea of dressing as favorite TV characters, Sitcoske simply shares photos of past events. "When people see what others have done, their imagination immediately takes off," she says. "Once they have a few ideas of their own, they get excited and start thinking about inviting friends and acquaintances."

Source: Mary Sitcoske, Secretary, Rotary Club of Pottsville, Pottsville, PA. Phone (570) 628-2969.
E-mail: Msitcoske@verizon.net

60. **Draw More Major Donors With Upper-level Membership Perks**

How does an organization ensure that upper-level memberships ($1,000 per year and up) are attractive to individuals of means? By providing at least one of three things, says Lauren Davidson, individual giving manager at the Contemporary Jewish Museum (CJM) of San Francisco, CA: access, recognition or opportunities for socialization.

Museum benefits offering access include priority admission, curator-led tours and invitations to exclusive receptions and artist events. Recognition-based benefits include an annual donor wall, newsletter mention and the option to underwrite major exhibitions and programs.

Benefits providing unique opportunities for socialization often focus on travel opportunities such as a tour of a donor's private glass collection or a tour of featured artists' Bay-area studios.

In offering upper-level benefits, Davidson says, they take into consideration that high-end donors may see the value of benefits differently than persons who give at lesser levels. Davidson mentions recognition as an example, noting that the desire for public acknowledgement often wanes at the highest levels of giving.

"People giving $10,000 to one institution are often giving it to several others," she says, "so recognition is not as important to them. We find it generally matters more to those in the $1,000 to $5,000 range because many of them give only to us."

Similarly, Davidson says, when offering social opportunities, museum officials often distinguish between on-site events (generally offered at $1,000 level) and off-site events (offered at $1,800 and up). Doing so, she says, provides a gradation of benefits that encourages individuals to upgrade memberships.

Regarding value benefits such as guest passes and gift shop discounts, she says that when it comes to upper-level donors, "these are not hugely compelling, but they're not meaningless, either," noting that members at the $1,000-plus

> **Strategy Moves Major Donors To Higher Giving Levels**
>
> To move individuals to higher (and more profitable) levels of membership, officials at the Contemporary Jewish Museum (San Francisco, CA) rely on a 12-member development committee.
>
> Comprising upper-level members and trustees, this committee offers a range of suggestions on events and benefits and also reviews renewing memberships monthly to decide whom to ask to move to a higher level of membership, says Lauren Davidson, individual giving manager.
>
> Because museum officials have found not asking to be one of the biggest obstacles to development, the majority of members are generally invited to upgrade. Staff at the museum's development office offers background research and coaching if needed, but it is almost always committee members who make the ask.
>
> "These are some pretty savvy fundraisers, and peer-to-peer solicitation has been a very effective tool for us," says Davidson, adding that around a quarter of donors increased their gifts by an average of 80 percent in 2009.

levels do make use of discounts and special sales.

The most important step to determining benefits that both reward members and encourage them to move up giving levels, she says, is understanding members' fundamental motivation. "We find about 75 percent of higher-level donors are mission-based, rather than benefits-based. The key, then, is structuring benefits to make sure those individuals feel involved with the institution in which they believe. It all comes back to building and strengthening relationships."

Source: Lauren Davidson, Individual Giving Manager, Contemporary Jewish Museum, San Francisco, CA. Phone (415) 655-7829.
E-mail: Ldavidson@thecjm.org

61. Discovering Fundraising Brilliance Through Block Parties

Interested in a creative way to raise funds? Host a block party benefit.

One organization that has broken fundraising ground through this type of event — and which today raises $1 million-plus annually through this method — is the Concern Foundation for Cancer Research (Los Angeles, CA). The 43-year-old organization, which has a mission of dedicating and raising grant funds to support worldwide cancer research, has become renowned for its block party fundraiser concept.

Started by 15 Los Angeles couples wishing to honor a friend battling cancer, the organization earned $18,000 in its first two years, and held its first unofficial block party in the gardens of a Bel Air estate. The event eventually transferred to other locations, including the world famous Rodeo Drive in Beverly Hills.

In July 2010, organizers hosted the 36th annual block party on the back lot of Paramount Studios. The event, which enlists the help of Los Angeles magazine as its media partner, cost $300,000 and grossed $1.4 million, earning a total of $1.1 million. All proceeds from the event go toward funding for 63 cancer researchers worldwide.

How did the organization grow the block party event to what it is today? Derek Alpert, foundation president, says the key elements include:

- Securing new participants from local restaurants (the event featured 11 new restaurants/caterers and beverage suppliers in 2010 totaling 63 food stations, at which the staffing and food were all donated).

- Changing the theme each year (2010's theme: circus).

- Involving interactive activities each year. The July 2010 event provided massages and manicures and featured a 70-table casino setting.

"It's important to keep it fresh, yet comfortable for the folks who come each year," Alpert says. "The event is casual, with no hotel rubber chicken dinner. It has become a piece of LA charity event culture. We give our funds efficiently and as promised to cancer research, and it is an event that is geared to all ages. It is very reasonably priced for all that the donors receive for their support."

One major component of such a large-scale event, he says, involves securing proper permits, insurance and other legal requirements beforehand. "Every city and state has specific requirements for permits for any fundraiser," he says. Also, block party hosts may be required to alert residents who may be affected by a block party that is held in their area.

Finally, Alpert says, have event liability insurance such as an umbrella policy to cover all vendors, as well as copies of vendor's liability insurance, which may be required by your insurance carrier.

Source: Derek Alpert, President, Concern Foundation for Cancer Research, Los Angeles, CA. Phone (310) 360-6100. Website: www.concernfoundation.org

Keys to Hosting a Profitable Block Party

Looking to have a profitable block party?

"Keep it fresh, keep it simple, keep it interesting," says Derek Alpert, president of the Concern Foundation for Cancer Research (Los Angeles, CA), which hosts block party benefits each year. Also, he says, "Put yourself in the donor's place as to what they should expect to receive based on what you would expect the event to be like if you were the guest."

"Above all," says Alpert, "never say no to any offer of help or donations. Try to make everything work unless it goes against best judgment or in keeping with the organization's mission (e.g., being a cancer research organization we would never take sponsorship from tobacco) and make the whole experience (planning, volunteer involvement and day of the event) fun for everyone involved."

Alpert cites nine key elements for a successful block party:

1. Organization.
2. Creativity.
3. Involving a large section of the community in terms of vendor participation.
4. Having a strong core of volunteers and one strong leader with vision.
5. Having a great theme.
6. Attracting all ages.
7. Offering great value for the donation/ticket price.
8. Covering all out-of-pocket expenses with sponsorships before the doors are open or the first tickets are sold.
9. Finding an honoree to help your organization raise funds and awareness outside of your own established donors. (The Concern Foundation chooses an honoree each year. Honorees are individuals who are committed to assist Concern reach its goal to raise $1 million-plus each year from its block party event.)

62. Fundraiser Hits Sweet Spot

How do members of the Mira Mesa High School Foundation (San Diego, CA) regularly gross $20,000-plus with a single event? Easy. They aim for people's stomachs.

"The Taste of Mira Mesa is a community-wide event showcasing the many ethnic restaurants found in our neighborhood," says Esther Alameddin, foundation president.

Some 15 to 20 restaurants take part every year, donating food and providing the staff to serve it. Though the event is well-established now, Alameddin says convincing restaurant owners wasn't hard even the first time. "They see the money spent as an advertising expense," she says. "Some even pass out special coupons to track how much business they create."

Leveraging business connections of another kind, the event is held in the interior courtyard of a local business. Tickets ($25) are sold at the door, but most of the 300-plus tickets are pre-sold to parents, foundation supporters, community members, and students of other area schools.

Student participation is an important key to the event's success, Alameddin says. In the past, the school culinary department provided and served a specially created meal. Currently, student volunteers pass out beverages, help set up and tear down equipment, and provide live music to complement the work of professional disc jockeys and emcees.

For foundations looking to produce a taste-of fundraiser, Alameddin recommends a strong, reliable committee structure.

"With so many people to coordinate, you need a committee for everything," she says. "Membership, tickets, preparing gift baskets, auctioning off the gift baskets, coordinating restaurants — everything benefits from more hands. But done right, it all leads to a fun and inviting experience."

Source: Esther Alameddin, President, Mira Mesa High School Foundation, San Diego, CA. Phone (858) 692-7662.
E-mail: Ealameddin@gmail.com

63. Successful Auction Strategies

With 17 years as a licensed auctioneer and a nonprofit client list that includes Make-A-Wish Foundation, the American Heart Association and more major names, Dawn Rose-Sohnly knows what it takes to make a nonprofit fundraising auction a success.

President and owner of Elite Consulting LLC (Maumee, OH), she shares some of her best advice for auction success:

❏ **Establish a contract and understand the legalities related to the event.** The contract should outline responsibilities of the auctioneer; bid assistants; who is collecting the money raised; whether the auctioneer is licensed and bonded; and who is providing the clerks, cashiers, and any other additional help at the auction. Be aware of your state's auction laws, as well as sales tax and license laws.

❏ **Provide Internet bidding.** If possible, incorporate online bidding during the live auction so online bidders participate in real time.

❏ **Plan ahead how minimum bids will be handled.**

❏ **Hire a professional auctioneer.** An experienced auctioneer knows the bid increment levels, knows how to encourage bidding and knows how to communicate with the audience.

❏ **Understand your audience.** If you're asking for $5,000 for a specific item, know you have someone in the room who will contribute that amount.

❏ **Use bid assistants/bid spotters** to help create excitement, encourage bidding, establish rapport and expedite the sale of items being sold.

❏ **Understand the auction software.** Make sure whoever is working with the software is familiar with it inside and out. If you do not have the auctioneer collect the funds raised, consider hiring a company such as Auction Pay to keep the checkout line moving.

❏ **End with a follow-up meeting.** Do so one week after the auction to discuss aspects that worked well, and those that need more attention.

Source: Dawn Rose-Sohnly, President & Owner, Elite Consulting LLC, Whitehouse, OH. Phone (419) 260-7673.
E-mail: dawn@elitebenefitauctions.com.
Website: www.elitebenefitauctions.com

Lightning Source UK Ltd.
Milton Keynes UK
UKOW012317110713

213588UK00006BA/244/P